First published in Australia in 2007 by
New Holland Publishers (Australia) Pty Ltd
Sydney • Auckland • London • Cape Town
14 Aquatic Drive Frenchs Forest NSW 2086 Australia
218 Lake Road Northcote Auckland New Zealand
86 Edgware Road London W2 2EA United Kingdom
80 McKenzie Street Cape Town 8001 South Africa

Ravidà, Natalia.
        Seasons of Sicily.

        Includes index.
        ISBN 9781741104592 (hbk.).

        1. Cookery, Italian - Sicilian style. I. Title.

        641.59458

Publisher: Martin Ford
Project Editor: Lliane Clarke
Designer: Tania Gomes
Production: Linda Bottari
Printer: Imago, Singapore

10 9 8 7 6 5 4 3 2 1

A cookbook created by generations of Sicilians

Natalia Ravidà inherited a love of food and olive oil from the legacy of her Sicilian ancestors. The family farm at La Gurra has been in the Ravidà family since the 1770s, when nobleman Antonio Ravidà married Maria Ferrantelli, a wealthy noblewoman who received the fiefdom of La Gurra as a dowry.

The estate lies in an area still devoted to farming and is dominated by a sixteenth century farmhouse overlooking the Mediterranean Sea. From this oasis of olives, grapes, fruit trees, wild herbs, vegetables and pastures comes *Seasons of Sicily*, a record of Natalia's favourite Sicilian dishes.

Born in Trento, in northeast Italy, attending school in Rome and Nairobi, Kenya, Natalia had a successful career as a print, radio and television journalist in Paris, London and Italy. Her renewed passion for Sicily saw her leave journalism and since 1991 she has promoted RAVIDA Extra Virgin Olive Oil around the world, moving to Sicily to work in the olive oil business. She lives in Mondello, outside Palermo, with her husband Giuseppe Spatafora and young son Alfredo.

Contents

The sixteenth century farmhouse, La Gurra.

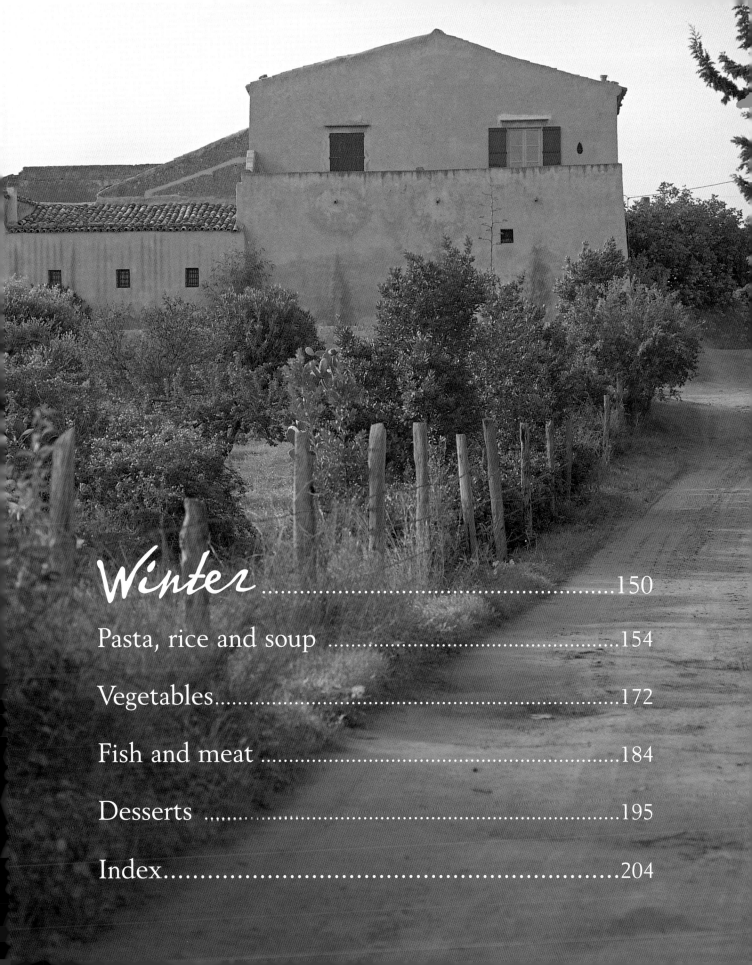

Winter

In the heart of the *Mediterranean*

An island

On first impressions, Sicily can be an intimidating country—its beauty often hidden away in enclosed courtyards or behind eternally shut windows.

This island that enchanted the Greeks, captivated the Arabs and the Normans and was preyed on by the Romans, Spanish, French and British, was always dominated, never its own owner. And so it shields itself away from newcomers.

If you persevere, you will find an island of great natural beauty, with an intricate history and unspoiled traditions.

The popular image of Sicilians from Francis Ford Coppola's *The Godfather* or the *La Piovra* TV series—dark-haired, ignorant and *mafiosi*—has given the island a reputation it does not need. Enormous amounts of money are now invested by the Sicilian government to promote the island for what it is: a land of sea, sun and culture.

Sicily is first of all a way of life: nostalgic, pessimistic, in love with itself, deeply rooted in a glorious past best revealed in Tomasi di Lampedusa's famous novel *The Leopard*. Yet, if Hamlet's dilemma was 'to be or not to be', a Sicilian's is 'to do or not to do'. Sicilians wait, as everything seems to be best resolved by time … which tends to mean everything remains the same.

Travellers will discover a surprisingly cosmopolitan people, unexpectedly blond and blue-eyed. A warm hospitality, rooted in impeccable etiquette. A landscape with a wealth of produce and an architecture that spans over 2500 years.

I had a very romantic vision of Sicily. I was a full-time journalist in London and whenever I arrived in the family home in Menfi, I could not help being captivated by its history and way of life. I gradually discovered a feeling of belonging. Dozing off on a deckchair in the courtyard on long summer afternoons, I then went back to my flat in London, running from one interview to another, wrapped up in hats and scarves with the constant rain as my dearest companion. This is how my transformation from journalist to olive oil and food enthusiast took place, one that led me to marry and settle permanently in Sicily.

A Sicilian villa

When you first step into the enclosed eighteenth century courtyard of Villa Ravidà you can't help but feel that here time has come to a halt. With its early-neoclassical columns reminiscent of the nearby temples of Selinunte, the house stands unaltered by time, by earthquakes and so far, by much needed restoration.

On each side of the portico, two Washingtonia palm trees sway in the wind. Planted when my father and his sister Maria were born, they mark the passing of time. Also the intensity of the wind. When the *scirocco* blows with all its might from Africa and the south-west, we watch them with apprehension, expecting them to receive their last blow.

A family legacy

My sisters and I certainly have had different upbringings. I was born in Trento, in northeastern Italy, a region with a great red wine tradition, now exported to La Gurra's vineyards. Patrizia, now in financial banking in Milan, was born in Catania whilst we lived in the beautiful town of Taormina, on Sicily's eastern coast. Nicoletta, the youngest, a lawyer, was born in Rome immediately after our return from Kenya. I always say that I have Sicilian DNA, an Anglo Saxon education and feel I belong wherever I happen to live. This combination allows me to survive in a sometimes restrictive Sicilian society.

As emigrating is often a necessity, upper class Sicilian families do not consider living abroad to study or achieve a career an improvement in status. When I moved to Sicily from London, everybody seemed to avoid what they saw as embarrassing questions (for them, obviously) about my life on my own and as a journalist. When I talked about our family estate, olives, vines or Sicily's beauty, I had a conversation on the right track.

Like a true Sicilian landlord, my grandfather, Luigi, lived off the harvests of the farm, enjoying yearly trips to fashionable locations in Europe. My grandmother, Natalia, whose name I inherited, had an independent, entrepreneurial spirit. In the 1930s—when women simply did NOT drive—she would take the wheel herself. She always had a new invention in hand. Had she lived in a country where ideas became realities, I am sure her life would have been different.

Both my grandparents loved to cook, even if their mutual epicurean interests resulted in the combination of opposite Sicilian cookery traditions, which I try to keep alive at Villa Ravidà. My grandmother contributed the more refined nineteenth century French–Sicilian baronial cuisine, while my grandfather provided a more earthy style of cooking. When I was a child, the house was run by my grandfather's staff and his very colourful cook, Joe—who had emigrated to the United States in the 1920s and returned to Sicily with gaudy gangster stories.

Joe made the most delicious *Carciofi fritti* and *Ragu di maiale* but when my grandmother visited, he suddenly disappeared. It was now time for *Fritto misto* or *Pizza rustica* and *Panzerotti* and a whole array of sweets like *Gelo di melone* in the summer, *Crema gialla o al cioccolato* or *Segreto della Dama*.

Out of this marriage of tastes and personalities came my father, Nicolo, who left Sicily to pursue a successful career as a civil engineer. When he married my mother, Ninny, she happily left Palermo to embrace my father's touring around Italy and abroad. She claims to have never walked into a kitchen before her wedding but has developed into a wonderful cook, instilling in us all the pleasure of good food.

Today in Menfi, entire days can go by in the kitchen cooking, just for the sake of passing time, an occasion to share time with family or friends. I have gathered many of the recipes that were once prepared by my grandparents and now by my mother, myself or my aunt Maria, in this book. I hope that while you cook them you can take pleasure in the taste of Sicily's seasons.

As the intensity of ingredients varies, we tend to balance ingredients with the eye, and then by smelling and tasting until that perfect combination is achieved.

Life at La Gurra

La Gurra has been in the Ravidà family since the 1770s, when one of my ancestors, Antonio Ravidà, married Maria Ferrantelli, a wealthy noblewoman who received the fiefdom of La Gurra as a dowry. The villa in Menfi, with its beautiful frescoed ceilings, was built by her father, Vincenzo Ferrantelli as their summer house. This is how the Ravidàs, a family that belonged to the nobility of Trapani since the 1200s, eventually moved to the town of Menfi.

The estate lies in an area still devoted to farming and is dominated by a sixteenth century farmhouse overlooking the Mediterranean sea. La Gurra has been a large estate in the past, an oasis of cork oak trees, olives, grapes and pastures.

Today, the estate is run organically with four main crops: grapes, olives for oil, table olives, lemons and our much adored vegetable garden. Because of my great love for olive oil, when I saw the beginning of a market for estate-bottled quality oils towards the end of the 1980s, I convinced my father to enter a new phase with direct marketing of the oil.

Olive trees are beautiful evergreens with silvery green leaves that give you a sense of peace and eternity, their trunks twisted and worn by time. The plants in the old olive grove are estimated to be over 400 years old and were probably grafted onto wild rootstock with local edible varieties such as Cerasuola, Biancolilla and Nocellara, which we still use to produce our oil.

Traditionally the harvest began after *I morti*, the celebration of the dead in the first week of November. Today, due to a warmer climate, it starts within the first days of October lasting for a good twelve weeks. Olive trees need relatively little care throughout the year but healthy, unblemished fruits are one of the initial steps to a good quality olive oil.

Olives are picked by hand and with vibrating rakes. As the drupes fall onto nets placed under each tree, they are gathered and cleaned of all leaves, put into crates and taken to our press. Here, they are washed and crushed at low temperatures with short cycles of extraction all within eight hours from picking. The oil is then stored at controlled temperatures.

Extra virgin olive oil is a highly perishable product that deteriorates in contact with oxygen, heat and light. So, from the very moment olives are picked, crushed into a paste and the oil extracted, a producer's main concern is to limit the damage provoked by oxidation. Great care must be taken when storing olive oil in your own home. Bottles must be kept away from heat—the stove -direct light and most of all should always be kept perfectly clean. The oil on the top of the bottle is the first to oxidise, contaminating the rest of the product. With time oils tend to lose their aroma and taste so they should ideally be used within a few weeks after opening.

Even though olive oil is the natural juice of the olive, its many classifications - extra virgin, virgin, olive oil—and prices confuse the consumer. In fact, today, it is only by learning to taste oils, to perceive its grassiness, its balance of pepper and bitterness that one can learn to detect a good from a bad oil. The rest is a matter of taste, as the many hundreds of olives in the world combine with the land and climate to produce oils with very different characteristics—just like wines.

The use of extra virgin olive oil is greatly encouraged, due to its high content of mono-unsaturated fatty acids and antioxidants, mostly detected in green and grassy oils. Those with very high contents are not only healthier but have a longer shelf life.

Extra virgin olive oil is certainly part of our culture and deeply rooted in our gastronomy. The opening of the market for quality oils in recent years has led to a new awareness that will encourage the production of higher quality oils—to give those who love it the pleasure of enjoying its wonderful taste and flavour.

As table olives must be unblemished and perfect in size, they have to be picked by hand. Some varieties are picked green, others, such as the *Giarraffa* shown here, when they are black.

My father shows Alfredo a centenarian cork oak tree at La Gurra. It takes seven years for the bark to develop into cork and be picked.

Spring

Although Easter marks the beginning of spring, it always seems to coincide with the return of true winter weather—rain and often a good shower of snow. This does not inhibit our urge to get out of the city and into the countryside.

At La Gurra, the olive trees and citrus groves are all in full bloom and wildflowers fill the countryside. Just the thought of the heat and drought that is about to arrive in summer makes the sight of them a cherished treasure.

Under both lemon and olive trees, after a downpour of rain, we pick wild asparagus, with their tinge of bitterness, which will find their way into pasta and *frittata* or be served with a simple fried egg. Spring is also the time for fresh fava beans, peas and wild fennel that feature in a wonderful stew called *Frittella*.

Green pastures make the best ricotta cheese of the year, used in *Pizza rustica* but also sumptuously in desserts like *Cassata al forno* or *Cannoli*.

It is also the time for tasty fish soups and tuna, which only appears in the markets in the month of May.

La Gurra: The olive grove (above) and (below) the road lined with ancient cork oak trees which connected Menfi to the farmhouse at La Gurra. The main building dates back to the sixteenth century.

Pasta rice and soup

Sfincione
Pizza with onions, tomatoes and anchovies

Sfincione belongs to popular cuisine. Its soft, well-risen dough is seasoned with a mixture of onions, anchovies, cheese and oregano, which makes plain pizza dough a sad affair in comparison. We started making it for end of harvest meals at the farm and it is now a staple of our 'lunch at the farm', alongside grilled sausages with wild fennel. It is ideal for a picnic or to take on a boat trip.

Serves 6

800g (1¾lb) plain flour
450ml (14 fl oz) water
40g (1½oz) yeast
30g (1oz) salt
1 large white or red onion (about 30g (1oz) in weight), finely sliced
½ cup white wine
500g (1lb) ripe peeled tomatoes
6 to 8 anchovies, according to taste
60g (2oz) freshly made breadcrumbs
60g (2oz) pecorino cheese, grated
8 tablespoons extra virgin olive oil
1½ tablespoons parsley, finely chopped
1½ tablespoons oregano
sea salt
black pepper

Warm the water to 37°C (98°F). Pour half the water into a cup and dissolve the yeast.

Sift the flour with the salt in a large bowl and gradually mix in the yeast, 2 tablespoons of olive oil and the remaining water. Knead for five to ten minutes, until all water is absorbed and dough is smooth and soft If using a food processor, mix for about five minutes at medium speed or until dough holds together and comes off the sides of the bowl. Punch a further minute by hand.

Grease a large bowl with a couple of drops of olive oil. Mould the dough into a slightly flattened ball, place it in the bowl and make a cross along the centre with a knife. Cover with a cloth and leave to set for two hours in a warm corner of the kitchen.

In the meantime, warm 6 tablespoons of olive oil in a medium sized pan, stir in the onions and sweat for 15 minutes with the lid on. Pour in the wine, reduce and add the chopped tomatoes, parsley, salt and a dash of pepper. Cover and cook for a further 10 minutes. Switch off and stir in the anchovy fillets.

Mix the breadcrumbs with the cheese and the oregano.

Knead the dough again for a couple of minutes. Grease a 30cm (12in) tin with olive oil and cover with the dough, stretching it to the sides of the tin. It should be about 1cm high.

Now season the *sfincione* by pushing the tomato mixture into the dough with your fingers, about every 3cms. Coat with the remaining tomatoes making sure seasoning covers dough up to the edges. Top with the breadcrumb and cheese mixture, coat generously with olive oil. Leave somewhere warm, possibly near a hot stove, for at least 1½ hours. It should raise to about three centimetres.

Warm oven to 220°C (450°F) Gas Mark 6.

Bake for about 20 minutes until bottom of the crust has a light golden hue.

Cut into squares and serve at room temperature.

Next page left: *Sfincione* is a well-seasoned pizza that
has been worked to raise almost like a French *brioche*.
Next page right: Time for a break at La Gurra.

Pizza rustica
Ricotta and salami pie in a sweet crust

This delicate pie with a ricotta cheese and salami filling combines with the mild sweetness of the pastry. We have it for Easter family gatherings, a time when ricotta cheese is at its best. We use wine instead of water to add extra flavour to the crust. *Pizza rustica* is ideally made a day in advance. Serve it as a main dish for a light lunch, a buffet or a picnic.

Serves 4

For the crust:
400g (12oz) of flour
50g (1¾oz) of sugar
¼ teaspoon vanilla
½ teaspoon of salt
150g (5oz) of butter, chopped
1 egg
½ cup dry white wine, approximately

For the filling:
500g (1lb) ricotta cheese, thoroughly drained
80g (3oz) salami
200g (7oz) provola piccante or a sharp cheese, finely chopped
¼ cup parmesan cheese, freshly grated
freshly ground black pepper

Make a shortcrust pastry—mix the flour with the sugar, vanilla, salt, butter and egg, adding white wine instead of water. Shape into a flat ball, wrap in plastic film and leave to rest in the fridge for at least half an hour.

Warm oven to 200°C (400°F) Gas Mark 5.

Cream the ricotta cheese with a fork and mix in the chopped cheese, salami and parmesan cheese. Season with pepper to taste. Line a 26 x 3cm (11in) baking tin with baking paper. Coat with butter and a bit of flour. Roll out the pastry to about ½cm (¼in) so as to cover the sides of the tin. Fill with the cheese and salami mixture. Cover with the remaining pastry, closing tightly around the edges. Prick top of the pastry with a fork to release moisture and bake for 45 minutes or until golden. Serve at room temperature.

Right: *Pizza rustica* wraps ricotta cheese with salami and a sharp cheese in a sweet crust. A great contrast.

Zuppa di pesce al brodo di verdure
Fish soup with vegetable broth

Serves 4

For the broth:
½ stalk of celery or beet or any other mild greens, a few leaves

6 tablespoons extra virgin olive oil
½ cup celery, diced
½ cup onion, diced
¼ cup carrot, diced
400g (12oz) potatoes, diced
1½ cup leeks, diced
a sprig of fresh thyme or rosemary
peppercorns
2 garlic cloves
800g (1¾lb) rock fish, scaled and gutted
½ cup white wine
140g (4½oz) pastina or spaghetti, chopped into 2cm (¾in) pieces
a pinch of saffron in powder

Bring 2 litres (3½ pints) of water to boil in a stockpot, add the celery stalk or other greens and simmer for about 20 minutes. Remove vegetables from broth with a slotted spoon.

Warm 4 tablespoons of olive oil in a saucepan and stir in the celery, onion, carrot and potatoes. Add a couple of spoons of broth and cook for about 5 minutes over low heat. Add the leeks, rosemary or thyme, a few peppercorns, one more ladleful of broth and cook for a further 5–7 minutes.

In a separate pan, warm 2 tablespoons of oil with the garlic cloves. Quickly stir in the fish with the wine, cover with more broth and cook, with a lid over medium heat for 10–15 minutes or until the fish is just about cooked.

Remove the fish from the saucepan and fillet carefully, taking out all bones and skin. Filter the fish broth and add to the soup base. Bring back to the boil and cook the pasta. By doing this the pasta will absorb all the flavour of the broth. Add the saffron and the fish just before taking off the heat. Thin with more vegetable stock, if necessary, and serve.

Linguine con asparagi selvatici
Linguine with wild asparagus

Wild asparagus differ enormously from domestic asparagus. They are long, thin and grow hidden by their spiny bushes. Searching for them can be an exhausting if rewarding experience, fuelled only by the thought of their delicious bitterness.

Serves 4
    1 bunch of wild or domestic asparagus, about 500g (1lb)
    1 small onion, finely chopped
    3 tablespoons extra virgin olive oil
    a pinch of saffron
    400g (12oz) pasta
    parmesan cheese, for serving

Pick off the asparagus tips and set aside. Break the stalks where soft and break into pieces.

Fill a small pot with salted water and boil the asparagus stalks until soft. Drain, reserving the water. Cream the stalks in a blender or chop very finely.

In a medium-sized pan, warm 4 tablespoons of olive oil and cook the onion until transparent. Add the asparagus tips, a couple of spoonfuls of asparagus water and cook until soft. Add the creamed asparagus, season with salt, a pinch of saffron and switch off.

In the meantime, bring a stockpot of salted water and any remaining asparagus water to the boil and cook the pasta. Drain, pour into a serving bowl and mix thoroughly with the asparagus. Serve with grated parmesan cheese on the side.

Ditali con zucchine e fiori di zucca
Ditali with zucchini flowers

When zucchini (courgettes) are in season, the greatest treat are their yellow flowers known as *fiori di zucca*. They go well with pasta, rice or in an omelette.

Serves 4

400g (12oz) zucchini (courgette) flowers
1 small spring onion (scallion), finely chopped
extra virgin olive oil
2 medium-sized zucchini (courgettes), sliced or finely chopped
½ cube of vegetable stock
sea salt
a pinch of saffron
400g (12oz) short pasta such as ditali or tagliatelle
parmesan cheese, freshly grated

Remove outside anther from zucchini (courgette) flowers. Dust with a cloth or wash with water just before cooking or they will wilt.

Warm 4 tablespoons of olive oil in a medium-sized pan, stir in the onion, a couple of tablespoons of water and cook until translucent and water has dried. Stir in the zucchini (courgette), the flowers, the stock and a good cup of water and cook over medium heat for about 10 minutes until zucchini (courgette) are soft and mushy. Add salt, saffron, a bit more olive oil, stir and switch off.

In the meantime, bring a stockpot of water to boil, add the salt and cook the pasta. Drain, pour into the pan and sauté for about 1-2 minutes over lively heat with the seasoning and a couple of spoonfuls of parmesan cheese. Transfer to a serving dish and serve with more parmesan cheese on the side.

Spaghetti con pesto di mandorle fresche
Spaghetti with fresh almond pesto

Almonds are usually picked in September at the end of the summer, but in late spring by mid-June they are fully formed. White, moist and with a mild flavour, they combine with new season's garlic and mint in this intensely fragrant pesto. Use packaged almonds if fresh ones are not available.

Makes 100g (3½oz) pesto

> 1 cup mint leaves, picked and dusted
> ¼ cup fresh almonds, peeled
> 2 tablespoons parmesan and 2 tablespoons pecorino cheese, grated
> 2 cloves of garlic
> ⅓ cup extra virgin olive oil
> 250g (8oz) tomatoes, peeled and sightly drained
> 400g (12oz) pasta, tubes, spaghetti or tagliatelle
> extra parmesan cheese or pecorino to serve

In a mortar or blender, mix the mint, almonds, cheeses, garlic and olive oil until almonds are coarsely chopped. Mix in the tomatoes and salt to taste.

In the meantime, bring a stockpot of water to boil add the salt and cook the pasta.

Drain, pour into a serving bowl and mix thoroughly with the pesto.

Serve with grated parmesan cheese on the side.

Vegetables

Frittella
Fresh broad bean, artichoke and pea stew

Frittella reigns in March when, at the end of the artichoke season peas, spring onions (scallions, shallots) and especially broad beans are just starting to appear. It is eaten as a starter, a side dish or a seasoning for pasta with different herb flavouring, depending on availability or mood.

Serves 4
   3 artichokes, perfectly cleaned as for Fried artichokes (see page 178)
   2 spring onions (scallion), sliced
   300g (9oz) broad beans, shelled
   300g (9oz) peas, shelled
   extra virgin olive oil
   sea salt
   a few leaves of either mint, parsley or wild fennel shoots, finely chopped

Warm 3 tablespoons of olive oil in a medium-sized saucepan and stir in the onion with the artichokes for a couple of minutes. Pour in a ¼ cup of water and cook over medium heat for about five minutes. Add the broad beans, the peas, a bit more water and cook until soft and water partially dried, about ten minutes. Cooking time will also depend on the tenderness of both peas and beans.

Season with salt, 3 to 4 tablespoons olive oil and the finely chopped herbs. If you are adding wild fennel shoots, finely chop about a tablespoon of the tender fronds and mix in five minutes before the end of cooking time.

Serve at room temperature.

Right: the fresh ingredients of *Frittella* before cooking.

Patate a spezzatino
Stewed potatoes with parsley

These potatoes cook slowly until almost creamy in texture and are then mixed with olive oil. Serve with a delicate fish such as *Sogliola al vino bianco* (page 129) or a more substantial *Salsiccia in padella* (page 190).

Serves 4
    800g (1¾lb) of starchy potatoes
    extra virgin olive oil
    sea salt
    shaving of nutmeg
    handful of fresh parsley or rosemary

Peel potatoes and cut into chunks. Put them in a medium-sized stockpot with about 1 cup of water, ¼ cup of olive oil and bring to the boil. Season with salt, cover with a lid, bring heat down to low and simmer until soft and water begins to dry, about 20 minutes.

When most potatoes have softened to a creamy consistency, add a shaving of nutmeg, a drizzle more of olive oil and the parsley or rosemary. Mix and switch off.

Serve either warm or at room temperature.

Insalata di pomodori, fagiolini, patate e cipolle
Tomato, string bean, potato and roasted onion salad

Pink onions are at their best around July. The variety found near Menfi is called *rosa di Partanna,* after the nearby town they come from. They can be up to 14cms (5ins) wide, flat on the edges and are renowned for their sweetness. In this dish they are oven roasted, giving this salad an exceptional taste. This is a regular lunch dish from late spring and throughout the summer. If you cannot find this variety use a sweet mild onion for this simple, yet delicious salad full of summer flavours.

Serves 4
   2 large white or pink onions
   400g (12oz) potatoes
   500g (1lb) string beans
   400g (12oz) ripe tomatoes
   sprinkle of oregano
   sea salt
   ½ cup extra virgin olive oil
   dash of red wine vinegar

Preheat oven to 200°C (400°F) Gas Mark 5. Place the onions on a baking tin and bake for about 30 minutes or until soft. Alternatively, peel and boil in water with a glass of white wine until soft, about 40 minutes. Drain and cut into thin slices.

   Boil potatoes in salted water until cooked, about 10 minutes depending on size. Drain, cool, peel and chop into cubes.

   Bring another medium-sized pot of salted water to the boil and cook the string beans until tender, about 7 minutes. Drain, rinse under cold running water and cut in halves if they are too long.

   Chop the tomatoes and mix in a serving bowl with the potatoes, string beans and the sliced onions. Season with the oregano, salt, olive oil and vinegar and serve at room temperature.

Next page: *Insalata di pomodori, fagiolini, patate e cipolle.*
Right: buying *rosa di Partanna.*

Fish, meat and eggs

Agnello al forno con le patate
Roasted lamb with potatoes

Sicilians only eat milk-fed lambs. If a lamb weighs more than 7kg (15lb) they consider it 'too strong' in flavour to be eaten. The other prerogative is that it must be extremely well cooked. This great delicacy is the traditional Easter lunch dish. Lamb is cut into small pieces and baked slowly with red wine until the meat is well browned but still tender.

milk-fed lamb, 7kg (14lb) max, chopped into 150g (5oz) pieces
extra virgin olive oil
2 large onions, halved
1½ kg (3lb) potatoes, peeled and coarsely chopped
black pepper
sage or bay leaves
red wine
sea salt

Preheat oven to 250°C (525°F) Gas Mark 7.

Place all the lamb pieces on a large oven tray so that they are spaced well apart and grease them with a little olive oil. Add the onions and potatoes. Season with a bit of pepper, the bay or sage leaves. Place in the oven and cook for first half hour at 250°C (525°F) Gas Mark 7. Turn the meat once, add the wine, lower heat to 150°C (300°F) Gas Mark 2 and cook for up to two hours, basting it regularly in its own juices adding more wine as needed. Season with salt halfway through cooking.

When meat is well roasted and starts to come off the bones, move lamb to a serving dish, scrape all juices from the pan, deglaze over high heat with a bit more wine or water and pour the gravy over the lamb.

Serve with the potatoes on the side.

Now that we no longer have our own sheep, we 'host' Nino Giarraputo. We get cheese and lamb from him.

Frittata con asparagi selvatici
Wild asparagus frittata

This frittata is left very thin and moist so that the eggs do not overpower the asparagus. No-one ever wants to miss out on a taste.

Serves 4

6 eggs
sea salt
4 tablespoons extra virgin olive oil
1 bunch of asparagus (preferably wild) cooked as per pasta recipe omitting the saffron (see Linguine with wild asparagus, page 26)

Beat the eggs in a bowl with a pinch of salt. Warm 4 tablespoons of olive oil in a 24cm (9in) non-stick pan and pour in the eggs. Spread over the asparagus and cook over low heat, allowing the raw egg to run to the base of the pan. Switch off the heat as soon as the base of the omelette has set, leaving the top runny and moist. It will keep cooking in its own heat.

Slide onto a serving dish, leaving creamy side on top and serve at room temperature.

Frittata con i fiori di zucca
Zucchini flower and onion frittata

This *frittata* is made with lots of onions. As soon as the sweet onions from Partanna are in season, I make sure I use them. Make this *frittata* thick and as moist as possible.

Serves 4
300g (9oz) of zucchini (courgette) flowers
⅓ cup extra virgin olive oil
1 large white onion, coarsely chopped
8 eggs
2 tablespoons parmesan cheese
sea salt

Remove the pollen-bearing sticky part of the stamen inside the flowers. Dust with a cloth or wash with water just before cooking or they will wilt.

Warm ⅓ cup olive oil in a 20cm (8in) non-stick pan and sweat the onion until transparent. Stir in the flowers, add just under ½ cup of water and cook over medium heat for 8–10 minutes until all water has dried.

In the meantime, beat the eggs with the parmesan cheese, season with salt and pour over the zucchini (courgette) flowers. Simmer over very low heat, letting the raw egg run to the base of the pan, until the omelette begins to set. Switch off the heat, leaving the top fairly moist. It will keep cooking in its own heat but remain creamy in the centre.

Turn onto a serving dish and serve at room temperature.

Shopping for artichokes in a Palermo vegetable market.

Ruota di tonno con crema di capperi
Tuna wheel with a caper and mint sauce

I made this impressive dish for one of my first buffet dinners after I married, to which I had invited some of my in-law's friends. One of the best waiters from our club, Circolo della Vela, had come in to help but when I showed him the tuna wheel ready to go into the oven he began mumbling and tried to convince me there was a catastrophe on the way. In fact, swordfish is more commonly used than tuna, but as it is often dry and everyone makes it, I am not very fond of it. Anyway, I was lucky and thanks to the topping of potatoes, my tuna wheel surprised and conquered all my highly discerning guests. Ask your fishmonger for a round, chunky slice of tuna of at least 12cm (5ins). If very fresh, it is best to keep it in the fridge for at least 12 hours before cooking.

Serves 12 people
   a 2½kg (5lb) slice of tuna, cut as above
   1 large new potato, cut into thin slices
   2 sprigs of mint
   2 cloves of garlic, optional, cut into 12 small wedges
   4 tablespoons extra virgin olive oil
   salt
   capers for decoration

   For the dressing:
   3 cloves of garlic peeled, optional
   3 cups extra virgin olive oil
   200g (7oz) of capers in sea salt
   1 tablespoon milk
   100g (3½oz) of fresh mint leaves
   rind from an organic lemon, finely shredded

Preheat oven to 180°C (350°F) Gas Mark 4.

Pat dry the slice of tuna.

Grease a baking tray with 1 tablespoon of olive oil and with half the potato slices form a circle the size of the fish piece.

With a larding needle, make six small holes on the top and bottom of the fish and fill them with a piece of mint wrapped around a wedge of garlic. Lightly grease the fish with a few drops of olive oil, season with salt, place it on top of the potatoes and top with the remaining potato slices. Add half a cup of water to the baking tray and cook for about 1½ hours, or about 25 minutes every 500g (1lb) or until cooked. Check regularly for moisture and add more water to baking tray if necessary.

When ready, discard all the potatoes and place the fish wheel on a round serving dish. Decorate with fresh mint leaves, capers and serve with mint and caper dressing (see below) on the side.

Salsa di menta e capperi
Mint and caper dressing

Capers are wild shrubs that grow amidst rocks near *i forti* where wild olives, cork oaks and small palm trees are surrounded by intensely flavoured wild thyme and fennel both, by now, in full flowering season. Salvino picks capers where my grandmother used to go horseback riding—*dove andava a cavallo sua nonna*—and brings them home in large woven baskets. We cure them with unrefined sea salt, in a large bowl, in a shaded ventilated corner of our kitchen patio, stirring them every two days for about a week until they lose their bitterness and turn from bright to a dark musky green. They are then stored in jars and topped with a bit more sea salt for later use.

Infuse the garlic in the olive oil for up to an hour in a small bowl covered with cling film to preserve flavour of the oil. Discard cloves.

Rinse capers with running water and leave for about 20 minutes in a bowl filled with water and a spoonful of milk. Leave longer if very salty. Rinse and drain well.

Chop the capers, the mint and the lemon peel and mix with the oil. Pour some dressing over the fish and serve more sauce on the side.

This can be prepared in advance and stored in a jar topped with olive oil.

Next page left: Capers are cured with sea salt in a shaded area until they begin to turn dark green. Next page right: Anchovies marinated in lemon and seasoned with olive oil are a refreshing starter or second course.

Alici al limone
Anchovies marinated with lemon

Smaller and more delicate than sardines, anchovies are in full season in spring. They make a fresh, light second course or starter.

Serves 4
    500g (1lb) of anchovies, scaled, gutted, main boned removed
    juice from one lemon, filtered
    ½ cup of extra virgin olive oil
    parsley or mint, finely chopped
    a pinch of fresh chilli, optional

Line the anchovy fillets in an oval dish and top with the juice of one lemon. Leave to marinate for about half an hour or until fish has turned white. Drain off the juice.

Line fillets on a serving dish, top with olive oil, sprinkle with parsley or mint and a dash of fresh chilli or pepper if you like a spicy taste.

Cover with cling film and refrigerate until ready to serve.

Desserts

Pecorelle di Pasqua
Almond Easter sheep

Pecorelle di Pasqua are always offered at Easter, the same way as *Nucatoli* are during Christmas festivities (see page 145). As the tradition to make them at home is almost lost, I asked the Mistretta cousins to kindly show me how to make *pecorelle*. The sheep moulds are only available in Sicily, but you can make them into small rounds, like cherries, or any shape you like, or use a biscuit cutter.

1kg (2lb) caster sugar
1kg (2lb) almond flour
½ tablespoon cocoa
moulds or cutter

In a medium-sized stockpot, mix the sugar with 250ml (½ pint) water over medium heat until well dissolved, about 10 minutes. Remove pot from heat and gradually add the almond flour, mixing thoroughly with a wooden spoon. Bring back to stove and stir until dough is well blended and no longer sticks to the sides of the pot. This should take about 5 minutes. Do not overcook.

Pour dough onto a marble surface to cool. It should be soft but it will harden as it cools.

Cut a quarter of the dough and roll into a cylinder. Slice off a third and carefully shape into the sheep mould. This does take experience and practice!

Once you have made all the almond sheep, mix the cocoa with a bit of water to a light creamy consistency. With a thin paintbrush draw the ears, mouth and face of the sheep and decorate the body. Traditionally a red ribbon is tied around the neck.

Torta di ricotta
Ricotta pie

Ricotta cheese is widely used in Sicilian sweets with wonderful results.

Serves 6

Pastry:
500g (1lb) flour
300g (10oz) sugar
pinch of salt
200g (7oz) butter, at room temperature
2 eggs and 1 egg yolk
¼ cup marsala
Filling:
700g (1½lb) ricotta cheese, thoroughly drained for at least 24 hours
250g (8½oz) sugar
10g (½oz) vanilla powder
100g (3½oz) black chocolate, finely chopped
1 tablespoon icing sugar
½ teaspoon cocoa powder
butter and flour to coat your tin

Make the pastry by mixing the sieved flour with the sugar and salt in a bowl or in a blender at low speed. Rub in the butter, chopped into pieces. Add one egg at a time, then the marsala and work dough until it is all incorporated. Shape into a ball, wrap with cling film and leave to rest in the fridge for about ½ an hour.

Preheat oven to 180°C (350°F) Gas Mark 4. In the meantime, sieve the ricotta cheese with a fork through a drum sieve and mix with sugar and vanilla until very smooth. Add a pinch of salt and the chocolate.

Coat a 26 x 3cm (10 x 1½in) pie dish with butter and flour, shaking off any excess flour or line with baking paper. Cut the pastry in half and shape into two rounds, one slightly larger than the other. Cover the bottom and sides of the pie dish with the larger round of pastry, lightly prick with a fork and fill with the ricotta cheese mixture. Cover with the second round of pastry, wrap tightly around the sides, make a small whole in the centre and bake in the oven for 45 minutes.

Leave to cool. Reverse mould onto a pie dish and sprinkle with icing sugar and a spoonful of cocoa powder before serving.

Cannoli
Cannoli

I first tasted *cannoli* a few years ago as I was taking a gourmet buyer from a large supermarket chain to Spinnato, one of Palermo's largest bakeries. The pastry chef simply could not believe I had never tried it in my entire life! I searched desperately for excuses as he thrust one into my hands and bid me to eat it. I do not regret it.

Fills 4 large or 8 small cannoli crusts

Filling:
150g (5oz) ricotta cheese, thoroughly drained
100g (3½oz) sugar
1 organic lemon, zested
1 pinch of cinnamon
1 tablespoon finely chopped black chocolate
Crusts:
150g (5oz) of flour
1 teaspoon cocoa powder
1 tablespoon of sugar
25g (½oz) butter
1 egg
1 tablespoon of white wine or marsala
extra virgin olive oil
icing sugar

Prepare the ricotta cheese filling as for the Ricotta pie (see page 56).

If you cannot buy ready-made cannoli crusts, set yourself to making them. Mix the flour with all the ingredients in a bowl or a blender until well combined. The dough must be smooth and elastic. Wrap in cling film and refrigerate for at least 30 minutes.

Roll out the dough fairly thin and cut into 10-12cm (4-5ins) squares. Wrap each sheet around a metal or bamboo cylinder, purposely made for cannoli.

In a deep frying pan, bring oil to frying temperature and fry the cannoli one at a time. Drip and cool on absorbent paper.

Carefully fill with the ricotta cheese, either by pushing it into the cannolo with the help of a knife or with a pipe. Sprinkle with icing sugar and serve.

Crema gialla o al cioccolatto
White and chocolate custard

When we were children, we would arrive in Menfi to find a fridge full of small glass bowls, some filled with white custard and others filled with chocolate custard. This tradition has continued into today's generation. I also use the white custard as a filling for Alfredo's birthday sponge cake or in the delicious Custard and strawberry tart (see next page).

200g (7oz) sugar
3 egg yolks
70g (2½oz) of wheat starch
1 litre (1¾ pint) of milk
zest of one lemon
cinnamon powder
1 tablespoon finely chopped dark chocolate
4 tablespoons dark chocolate cocoa
about 14 spongy biscuits, optional

In a stockpot, mix the sugar with the eggs.

Pour the wheat starch in a separate bowl and gradually add about a third of the milk, whisking constantly until creamy. Add to the sugar and eggs and incorporate all the milk. Cook over medium–high heat, stirring with a wooden spoon, until custard reaches a creamy consistency—about 4 minutes. Switch off the heat as soon as custard reaches the first boil or coats the back of the spoon. Use half the mixture for the white custard and half for the chocolate custard.

For the white custard, add the zest of lemon and leave to infuse for a few minutes. Then pour custard either into a glass bowl or into individual bowls. Once cooled and settled, sprinkle with a dash of cinnamon and finely chopped chocolate.

For the chocolate custard, pour the cocoa into a separate bowl and gradually whisk in a cup of custard. Add this mixture to the remaining custard pot and mix until well blended. As above, pour into a bowl or individual serving bowls and top with finely chopped chocolate.

You may also put biscuits such as *pavesini* in the bottom of the bowl before topping with the custard. The custard keeps in the refrigerator for several days.

Note: If preparing this for the Strawberry tart, increase wheat starch to 80g or even 100g (3-3½oz) depending on how thick you wish the custard to be.

Crostata di crema gialla e fragole
Custard and strawberry tart

This tart is so popular, both with our American and Australian guests, that I had to share it. My mother claims that the addition of suet—that she keeps reading about in all the old family recipes—makes the pastry much tastier.

Serves 4

For the crust:
250g (8oz) flour
125g sugar
pinch of salt
125g butter or half butter, half suet
1 egg

For the custard:
Make ½ litre of white custard as in Crema gialla (see page 58) using
80–100g (3½–3oz) wheat starch
600g (1¼lb) strawberries
½ tablespoon of sugar
a few drops of lemon juice

Make the pastry by mixing sifted flour with the sugar and salt in a bowl or in a blender at low speed. Rub in the butter, chopped into pieces. Add the egg and work dough quickly incorporating all ingredients. Shape into a ball, wrap in cling film and leave to rest in the fridge for about half an hour.

Preheat oven to 180°C (350°F) Gas Mark 4.

Coat a 26 x 3cm (11in) pie dish with butter and flour, shaking off any excess flour or line with baking paper. Stretch the pastry over the pie dish, lightly prick with a fork and cover with baking beans. Bake in the oven for 30 minutes or until golden. Place on a rack to cool.

In the meantime, remove stalks from the strawberries, cut them into quartered wedges and season with the sugar and a few drops of lemon juice.

Shortly before serving, fill the tart case with the custard and top generously with the strawberries.

Summer

Tenerumi and *zucchini lunga* for a light yet tasty meal in a hot summer evening.

Fresh garlic is knitted into a *treccia* or plait.

Sicilian summers are hot and getting hotter, with long periods seeing temperatures above 35°C (95°F). As the sun begins to set, my mother and I go to the organic vegetable garden at La Gurra to get a breath of cool air and pick vegetables for the evening dinner. Being close to the sea, sunsets at La Gurra are intensely red with the colours of nearby Africa as the sun plunges into the westernmost coast of Sicily. At this time of the year, the orchard is filled with the scent of basil and mint, with eggplants (aubergines), tomatoes, plenty of red and yellow peppers and a typical Sicilian green *tenerumi* and its long fruit *zucchina lunga*.

Back in Menfi at Villa Ravidà, the thick ancient walls of the house offer solace from the strong heat. At dusk, we move outside. The north facing courtyard, the *terrazzino di papà*, a little terrace on the southern façade of the house, fills with friends seeking solace from the heat, in search of a hopeful breeze, which, if luck prevails, will arrive early evening.

These gatherings are no more than an excuse for sharing time together, sitting on 1920s deckchairs, drinking martinis or glasses of ice cold white wine garnished with a mint sprig. From a legacy of hundreds of years of Spanish domination, dinner is never even mentioned before nine. It is only then, that my mother casually asks if anyone would like *qualcosa da mangiare*, something to eat. No-one ever refuses.

As the party moves to the *cortiletto* for dinner, a *Pasta con i tenerumi* or *Pomodoro crudo e melanzane* is usually followed by mouthwatering *Parmigiana, Involtini di melanzane con la béchamel* or a *Peperonata*, leaving everyone entirely satisfied. The variety of ways in which the same simple ingredients are used highlights the creativity of Sicilian cuisine.

Pasta, rice and soup

Pennette con gamberi e calamari
Pennette with prawn and calamari

Pasta with seafood is not highly regarded in the Ravidà family, especially by my father who claims it is not part of Sicilian tradition. Probably out of a sense of contradiction, my mother and I furtively develop recipes that we exchange regularly, never write down and have to create anew every time. When she makes a good pasta with seafood she claims it is my recipe. When I make a successful one, I maintain she inspired me. This recipe sums up summer pastas with seafood.

Serves 4

    600g (1¼ lb) medium-sized pink or rock prawns (shrimps)
    ½ cup (4fl oz) extra virgin olive oil
    4 garlic cloves
    1 pinch crushed red fresh or dried chillies
    dry white wine
    2 tablespoons flat parsley, finely chopped
    4 cherry tomatoes or 1 medium-sized ripe tomatoes, diced
    300g (9oz) fresh calamari, cut into rounds and chopped into 2-3cm strips
    salt
    freshly ground pepper
    400g (12oz) pennette lisce or linguine

Separate heads from prawn (shrimp) tails. Remove shells from tails and keep heads with their juices.

Heat 3 tablespoons of olive oil with 2 of the garlic cloves and a pinch of red chillies in a medium-sized pan over medium heat, until garlic turns translucent. Add the shrimp (prawn) heads, a dash of the white wine, and sauté over high heat. Cook until heads change colour, about three minutes. Switch off. Strain through a vegetable mouli set over a bowl and reserve the juices for later.

Finely chop the parsley stems and leaves separately.

Choose a medium-sized sauté pan where you can later mix in the pasta, heat 4 tablespoons of the olive oil and simmer the remaining 2 garlic cloves and the parsley stems for a couple of minutes. Put in the tomatoes and cook over medium heat until they have softened. Now add the calamari and a dash of wine over high heat. Lower heat, season with salt and a bit of pepper and cook for about five minutes. Add the prawns (shrimps). Stir and cook until prawns (shrimps) are ready, for about four minutes according to size, being careful not to overcook them. Now, add prawns (shrimps) juices, the parsley leaves (leaving a teaspoon for final topping), mix and switch off. Leave uncovered to prevent prawns (shrimp) from cooking further.

In the meantime, bring water to boil in a large stockpot. Add the salt and cook the pasta. Drain the pasta, add to the fish sauce and toss over high heat for about one minute. Check density—it should have a runny creamy consistency—and add a drizzle more olive oil if needed.

Pour into a large serving oval dish, sprinkling with a little more parsley for garnishing. Serve immediately.

Tortiglioni al pomodoro crudo, melanzane e basilico
Tortiglioni with raw tomatoes, eggplant and basil

When we were children our family owned a house in Taormina with a breathtaking view over the volcano of Etna and the whole of the eastern coast of Sicily. Because of the volcanic soil, tomatoes and all other produce from that area is of excellent quality. My mother prepared this pasta almost every day before going to the beach, ready for us when we returned starving. Use sweet, well-ripened plum tomatoes and ideally use with baked ricotta *(ricotta infornata),* unique to the eastern coast of Sicily.

Serves 4

400g (12oz) pasta—tortiglioni, rigatoni or penne lisce
2 medium-sized eggplant (aubergine), about 400g (12oz),
    cut into 2-cm cubes
2 cups (4fl oz) extra virgin olive oil for frying
2 garlic cloves, whole
10 fresh basil leaves
500g (1lb) ripe plum tomatoes
freshly ground black pepper
6 tablespoons freshly grated parmesan cheese, ricotta infornata or pecorino

Fry the eggplant as for Caponata (see page 83) and set aside to drain.

Bring water to the boil in a small stockpot and blanch the tomatoes. Peel and dice.

In a large serving bowl, mix the tomatoes with about ½ cup of olive oil, garlic, a pinch of salt and some pepper.

Bring water to boil in a large stockpot, add the salt and cook the pasta. When it is *al dente*, drain and mix with the tomatoes, add the eggplants, basil and some more olive oil if needed. Mix in the cheese or reserve it for the table. This pasta can also be eaten at room temperature.

Spaghetti con i ricci
Spaghetti with sea urchin roe

Sea urchins have a delicate sea flavour. Otherwise, the salmon coloured roe is scooped out of the shell and used as a delicious seasoning for spaghetti. There are two schools of thought on the use garlic—should it be used or not I think it adds to the flavour and a small pinch of chilli does not do any harm. Outside of Sicily, fish markets sell trays of fresh roe and some Spanish stores sell packaged sea urchin roe.

Serves 4

1 cup sea urchin roe (from about 80-100 sea urchins or bought)
400g (13oz) spaghetti
¾ cup (6fl oz) extra virgin olive oil
3 garlic cloves, optional
1 tablespoon flat parsley, finely chopped
sea salt

If you have caught fresh sea urchins, slit them in half with a knife wearing thick rubber gloves and scoop out roe into a glass bowl. Keep refrigerated or freeze if not using on the same day as they will 'melt' after a few hours.

Bring a large stockpot of salted water to boil and cook the spaghetti.

In the meantime, gently warm the olive oil in a small skillet with the garlic and simmer over a very low heat until transparent, without frying. Switch off and discard the garlic cloves.

Drain the spaghetti, reserving a cup of pasta water. Pour the spaghetti into a large serving bowl, mix well with the olive oil, the parsley and a spoonful of cooking water, if necessary, to obtain a creamy mixture. Add the roe, mix and serve immediately.

Insalata di grano
Wheat berry salad

In Roman times, Sicily was the barn of Europe and the quality of its wheat was renowned throughout the Empire. Wheat is harvested in the first week of June, filling the air with the unique scent of freshly mown hay. The countryside changes overnight from a lush green to a golden yellow, bringing the last days of spring straight into summer. I always have some wheat berries put aside for this fresh summer dish, considered a great novelty amongst Sicilian guests who eat wheat only as a sweet, as in Cuccia (see page 144). A wheat berry is the unprocessed wheat seed, rich in fibre, vitamins and minerals. You can use barley as an alternative.

Serves 4

250g (8oz) wheat berries or barley
3 garlic cloves
¾ cup (6fl oz) extra virgin olive oil
300g (10oz) ripe tomatoes, finely diced
8 fresh basil leaves, or alternatively flat parsley
8 fresh mint leaves
1½ tablespoons sea salt
pepper, freshly ground

Soak the wheat berries in a bowl covered with water for 24 hours and renew water at least every twelve hours.

Wash the wheat thoroughly with plenty of water and clean out any twigs. Cover with at least 6 cups of water in a medium-sized stockpot and add 1 tablespoon of salt. Bring to the boil, lower heat to a gentle simmer, cover with a lid and cook until grains are tender for about 2-2½ hours or until soft.

When the wheat is cooked, drain and pour in a serving bowl. Season with half the olive oil, a garlic clove and leave to cool or refrigerate overnight. This salad is best if made at least half a day in advance for all the flavours to mix. Refrigerate as wheat goes off easily. Combine the tomatoes with the 2 remaining garlic cloves, basil and mint and season with the remaining olive oil and pepper. Mix with the wheat. Adjust the salt, remove the garlic and serve at room temperature.

Pasta con i tenerumi
Mild greens soup with chopped spaghetti and primosale

Tenerumi are one of summer's most popular greens in Sicily but are unknown elsewhere. They are the tender leaves of *zucchina lunga*—a Sicilian variety of summer squash. Slightly velvety when raw, they are very mild in taste and grow in great quantities, spreading along the ground. This pasta soup is served warm or at room temperature.

Serves 4

300g (9oz) tenerumi leaves or any mild green leaves
300g (9oz) ripe globe tomatoes, chopped
⅓ cup (2½fl oz) extra virgin olive oil
4 garlic cloves
8 fresh basil leaves
200g (7oz) spaghetti, chopped or broken into 3cm pieces
½ cup (3oz) mild pecorino or parmesan cheese, grated or
    caciocavallo cheese finely diced
sea salt
freshly ground black pepper

In a medium-sized stockpot, bring 1½ litres (3 pints) of water to boil. Add salt and cook the tenerumi or other mild green leaves until soft, about 10 minutes. Scoop with a slotted spoon onto a medium-sized serving bowl and chop finely. Reserve water in a glass container if not using straight away, as it turns black with time.

Bring water to boil in a small stockpot and blanch the tomatoes. Peel and chop into 1cm cubes. In a medium-sized saucepan, warm 4 tablespoons of olive oil, add the garlic cloves and simmer for 2 minutes until transparent without burning. Add the tomatoes and cook until wilted, for about 5 minutes. Season with salt, a little bit of pepper and set aside.

In the meantime, bring vegetable water back to the boil adding some more if not enough. Cook the spaghetti *al dente*. Drain the pasta with a slotted spoon, reserving the water, and add to the tomatoes. Mix over heat for one minute and season with the basil.

Combine the pasta with the vegetables and the tomatoes, season with olive oil and mix. Leave to cool. Just before serving, add up to 1 litre (2 pints) of the vegetable water, according to taste and top with the cheese.

Tenerumi leaves are mixed with sautéed chopped tomatoes, a couple of cloves of garlic and spaghetti, traditionally chopped by hand in a kitchen cloth.

Minestra di zucchina lunga
Summer squash with oregano and olive oil

Zucchina lunga grows from the tenerumi plant. It has a very light green skin, which is peeled off and is similar in texture to summer squash. Its mild taste in this dish is enhanced by the sweetness of the onions and the cheese. My mother considers it a dish for *malati di stomaco* (people with weak stomachs) but my husband, my sister Patrizia and I are extremely fond of it. Erica De Mane, a food writer from New York, tells me both *zucchina* and *tenerumi* are available in specialty greenmarkets in the East coast during summer months and that her father used to grow them. If you know any Sicilians, ask them for both these vegetables. They might look at you in awe or think you are searching for the humblest of Sicilian vegetables. Don't let them put you off.

Serves 4
- 600g (1¼lb) zucchina lunga or a mild summer squash, peeled and cut into 4cm pieces
- 1 medium red onion, coarsely sliced
- 3-4 tablespoons extra virgin olive oil
- sea salt
- ½ teaspoon dried oregano
- ½ cup (3oz) caciocavallo cheese, finely chopped or freshly grated ricotta salata (a Sicilian variation on ricotta)

Bring about 300ml (10 fl oz) of water to boil in a medium-sized stockpot.

Add the zucchina and onion, cover and cook over medium heat, about 8 minutes. Remove lid to dry off excess water, season with the salt, the olive oil and oregano. Cook for a few more minutes or until soft.

Pour onto a wide bowl, top with the cheese and serve warm or at room temperature.

Spaghetti con salsa e melanzane fritte
Spaghetti with tomato sauce and fried eggplant

This is Sicily's most common summer dish and no-one seems to tire of it. Its success depends on the quality of the tomato sauce, which should be homemade with very ripe, sweet tomatoes. Sometimes, a pinch of sugar is added to get rid of any acidity. In the summer, fried eggplant (aubergine), either in cubes or slices depending on the type of pasta used, topped with fresh basil or mint give it a different twist every time. As Sicilians will always have fresh salsa ready, this is a great last minute dish and it will taste different every time you make it.

Serves 4
    400g (12oz) spaghetti, ditalini or caserecce
    3 cups (24 fl oz) tomato sauce/Salsa di Pomodoro (see page 88)
    1 medium eggplant (aubergine), about 300g (9oz), cut into 3cm slices if
        using spaghetti, or cubes if using other types of pasta.
    ½ cup parmesan cheese, or ricotta infornata, freshly grated
    8 fresh basil or mint leaves
    sea salt

Fry the eggplant (aubergine) as in Caponata (see page 83), or sliced as in Parmigiana (see page 82) if making spaghetti, and leave to drain.

Bring a medium-sized stockpot with salted water to boil. Cook the pasta and drain thoroughly. Pour back into stockpot and mix with the tomato sauce, the eggplant and half the cheese. Stir over medium-high heat for under a minute and switch off. Add half the basil or mint and pour onto a large round serving bowl.

Top with remaining basil or mint and serve with cheese on the side.

Pasta fritta
Fried pasta

Whenever pasta is left over, the next day it is fried and turned into a delicious *pasta fritta*, fried pasta. This works with any leftover cooked pasta, but especially well with *Spaghetti con salsa e melanzane fritte* (see page 74). Everyone claims it is dead easy to make. I am not of the same opinion, but this is how I manage to get a crunchy parmesan crust.

Serves 4
 ¼ cup extra virgin olive oil
 1½ cups freshly grated parmesan cheese
 400g (12oz) any leftover cooked pasta or
     leftover Spaghetti con la salsa e melanzane fritte (see page 74)

Warm half the olive oil in a medium-sized, non-stick sauté pan. Keep heat low and add half of the grated parmesan. As soon as it begins to sizzle and form a light crust, add the pasta. Flatten well with a spatula, cover with a lid and turn heat to medium low. Cook for at least fifteen minutes, checking crust regularly for consistency. Lower heat if it starts to brown too much.

When the parmesan has turned a nice golden brown, turn pasta onto a large plate. Pour remaining olive oil onto the pan, add remaining parmesan, add the pasta and start the process again to cook the other side of the pasta. Cook for a further 10-15 minutes or until it forms a crust on the other side.

Serve warm, crusty side up.

Vegetables

Pomodori ripieni
Tomatoes stuffed with toasted breadcrumbs, capers and basil

Serve these stuffed tomatoes as a side dish for meat or fish or with a combination of vegetables.

Serves 4

4 ripe tomatoes, about 5cms in size, halved horizontally
extra virgin olive oil
1 clove of garlic
3 anchovy fillets
1 tablespoon salted capers, rinsed in water and milk and finely chopped
1 tablespoon finely chopped flat parsley
½ cup breadcrumbs
sea salt

Remove seeds from tomatoes and leave to drain upside down in a colander set over a plate for about 15 minutes.

In a small iron pan, heat 3 tablespoons of olive oil with the garlic. Add the parsley, capers and anchovy fillets and mix in the breadcrumbs. Stir over medium heat until well mixed and gently toasted. Mixture must be quite moist with the olive oil or it will taste dry—adjust with another spoonful or two of olive oil and salt if necessary.

Warm oven to 200°C (400°F) Gas Mark 5.

Cover a baking tray with baking paper and grease with a few drops of olive oil. Fill each tomato half with a spoonful of the breadcrumbs and place on the baking tray. Bake tomatoes for about 30 minutes, or until skin begins to crease and toast. Serve warm or at room temperature.

Involtini di melanzane con la béchamel
Eggplant rolls with béchamel sauce

The thin, dark-skinned variety of eggplant (also used for *Caponata* see page 83) are at the base of these delicious eggplant rolls. Its pulp is somewhat drier than that of the light purple variety and remains crunchier during frying. Its slightly bitter skin offers a pleasant contrast with the béchamel and the tomato sauce. It is a classic summer evening dish in Menfi and it can be made in advance. Use any extra béchamel sauce for a few *Crocchè di latte* [see page 170].

Serves 4

3 medium-sized dark skinned eggplants (aubergines), about 600g (1¼lb), thinly sliced lengthwise, just under 1cm.
sea salt
4 cups extra vergin olive oil
1 cup tomato sauce/Salsa di pomodoro (see page 88)
fresh basil leaves for garnish
For the béchamel sauce:
50g (2oz) butter
50g (2oz) plain flour
½ litre (¾ pint) milk
3 tablespoons freshly grated parmesan cheese

Arrange the eggplant slices in a large bowl and cover with salted water. Leave to sit for ½ an hour to eliminate the bitter moisture and prevent them from absorbing too much olive oil when frying.

To make the sauce: Melt the butter in a medium saucepan over medium heat. Whisk in the flour and mix until a paste is formed. Gradually add the warmed milk until thoroughly combined.

Cook over medium heat stirring constantly until boiling point and switch off. Stir in 4 tablespoons of parmesan, add salt and set aside to cool.

Drain the eggplant slices and pat dry with a clean kitchen cloth.

Heat at least 2 cups of olive oil in a 25cm (10in) sauté pan with high sides over medium-high heat and bring to frying temperature. Add a single layer of the slices and cook until golden on both sides, reducing the heat if oil begins to burn or the eggplants colour too quickly.

Transfer the cooked slices to a colander set over a plate to drain off any excess olive oil. Repeat until all of the eggplant slices are cooked. If more olive oil is needed, add to empty pan and bring to frying temperature before cooking a new batch.

Preheat the oven to 200°C (400°F) Gas Mark 5.

Arrange the eggplant slices on a flat surface. Place a small amount (1–2 teaspoons) of the béchamel on one end of each slice and roll the eggplant around it. Arrange the eggplant rolls tightly in a 30cm (12in) oven-proof serving dish. Spoon the tomato sauce over the eggplant and sprinkle with the remaining 3 tablespoons of parmesan.

Bake until heated through, about 20 minutes.

Garnish with the basil and serve warm or at room temperature.

Parmigiana di melanzane
Eggplant parmigiana

Parmigiana is a traditional dish in Sicily and, in some parts, hardboiled eggs, potatoes and even mozzarella cheese are added. My mother's recipe is simple and uses the softer globe eggplant cut into fairly thick slices, which maintains the full eggplant flavour.

Serves 4
  1kg (2lb) globe eggplant (aubergine), cut into thick slices, about 2cms
  sea salt
  350ml (12 fl oz) tomato sauce/Salsa di pomodoro (see page 88) or passata
  250g (8oz) parmesan cheese, freshly grated
  2 cups extra virgin olive oil for frying
  1 sprig of basil leaves

Arrange the eggplant slices in a large bowl. Cover with salted water and leave for about half an hour. Drain and dry well with a kitchen cloth.

Heat at least 2 cups of olive oil in a medium-sized frying pan over a high heat and bring to frying temperature. When the olive oil is hot, add one layer of eggplant slices. Fry over high heat, turning once, until golden on both sides—about 7 to 10 minutes. Reduce heat if olive oil begins to smoke or slices burn. Transfer slices to a colander set over a plate to drain off excess olive oil. Cook all the eggplants this way, making sure there is always plenty of oil in the frying pan.

Preheat oven to 200°C (400°F) Gas Mark 5.

Coat a 24cm (9in) round oven dish with two spoonfuls of the tomato sauce. Cover with a layer of eggplant slices, 4 tablespoons tomato sauce, 4 tablespoons cheese and 4 basil leaves. Add another layer of eggplants, tomato sauce, cheese and basil leaves and continue until all the eggplants are used. It should make about four layers. Sprinkle with the remaining cheese and bake for about 20 minutes or until it is slightly crusty on the sides.

This dish can be served warm, at room temperature or it can be frozen for later use. Top with fresh basil leaves before serving.

Caponata di melanzane
Sweet and sour eggplant stew with pears

Every household in Sicily has their own favourite version of *caponata*—a dish with Spanish origins, some include octopus. *Caponata* tastes better the next day. It is usually made in large quantities and stored in glass jars for winter. Serve as a starter or a side dish.

Serves 4

600g (1¼ lb) dark skinned eggplant (aubergine), cut into 3cm cubes
sea salt
2 cups extra virgin olive oil for frying
2 celery stalks, cut into 2cm dice
2 large onions, coarsely chopped
40g (1½oz) capers cured in salt, thoroughly rinsed
100g (3½oz) green olives in brine, rinsed, pitted and chopped in halves
2 small pears, cut in quarters
½ cup red wine vinegar
1 tablespoon sugar
½ cup tomato sauce/Salsa di pomodoro (see page 88)
6 fresh mint leaves, optional

Arrange the eggplant cubes in a large bowl. Cover with water, sprinkle with salt and leave for about ½ hour. Drain and dry well with a kitchen cloth.

Heat at least 2 cups of olive oil in a medium-sized frying pan over a high heat and bring to frying temperature. When the olive oil is hot, add one layer of eggplant cubes. Fry over high heat, turning once, until golden on both sides—about 7 to 10 minutes. Reduce heat if olive oil begins to smoke or cubes burn. Transfer cubes to a colander set over a plate to drain off excess olive oil. Cook all eggplants this way making sure there is always at least 2–3cms (1in) of oil in the pan.

Pre-cook the celery until soft in boiling salted water and drain.

In a separate, similar sized skillet, warm 4 tablespoons of the olive oil and stir fry the onions over medium-high heat until transparent for about 5 minutes. Add the celery, pears, capers and olives. Allow flavours to mix for a couple of minutes and stir in the tomato sauce and the eggplant. In a cup, mix the sugar with the vinegar until dissolved and pour over the vegetables. Let it evaporate over high heat for a minute, mix and switch off. Pour in a serving dish and leave to rest for at least 24 hours. Top with mint leaves before serving and serve at room temperature. This dish can be kept in the fridge for a few days.

Peperonata
Capsicum stewed with tomatoes, onions and mint

There was always a *peperonata* with its sprigs of fresh mint ready for us when we stayed in Taormina. We usually had it for lunch, after a plate of pasta, as a cold second course.

Serves 4

4 large red and yellow capsicum (peppers), skinned and filleted
extra virgin olive oil
2 medium-sized onions, thinly sliced
2 tablespoons white wine vinegar
3 medium-sized ripe tomatoes, skinned and chopped into quarters
1½ teaspoons sea salt
10 fresh mint leaves

Warm oven to 200°C (400°F) Gas Mark 5.

Place peppers (capsicums) on oven rack and cook for 40 minutes, or until skin begins to wrinkle.

Remove peppers from the oven and put them in a closed plastic or paper bag for at least half an hour or until cool. The moisture released will make peeling easy. Peel off the skin, remove stem and all the seeds. Break up into fillets and place in a colander to drain off excess liquids.

Warm 4 tablespoons of olive oil in a medium-sized pan and cook the onions until transparent—3 to 5 minutes. Add the vinegar and let it evaporate over high heat for a couple of minutes. Stir in the tomatoes and then the peppers. Add about half a cup of water, cover with a lid and cook over slow heat for 10 to 15 minutes, stirring occasionally. Season with salt, a few mint leaves, a bit more olive oil and pour onto a serving dish.

Serve at room temperature and decorate with fresh mint leaves before serving. It can be made up to a day in advance.

Insalata di pomodoro e cipolle
Tomato salad with onions, oregano and capers

During hard times, farmers often ate just bread and onions. Today raw onions are rarely appreciated by well-to-do Sicilians, as they are still associated with poverty. Red onions are usually marinated in vinegar to enhance their flavour before being mixed with tomatoes and capers for a tasty tomato salad.

Serves 4

1 large red or pink onion, thickly sliced
red wine vinegar
sea salt
600g (1¼ lb) ripe plum tomatoes, chopped into cubes
¼ cup salt cured capers, thoroughly rinsed
1½ teaspoons oregano
extra virgin olive oil

Slice onion and marinate in a bowl with vinegar and salt for about fifteen minutes. Drain and squeeze off excess vinegar.

Toss the tomatoes in a medium-sized serving bowl with the capers, onion, oregano, salt, a dash of vinegar and olive oil. Mix well and serve.

This can be prepared up to an hour in advance.

Next page left: *Peperonata* was always ready for lunch when we were children. It can also make a seasoning for pasta.
Next page right: A salad with sun ripened tomatoes, onions and capers. Red onions are sweet and marinated in vinegar or water and salt if added raw to a salad.

Salsa di pomodoro
Tomato sauce

My husband's whispered complaint is that since he has been married he eats a great variety of foods but, 'if only I could have *un piatto di pasta con la salsa* (a dish of pasta with tomato sauce) a bit more often'. By mid-August, when the heat and the lack of water have ripened tomatoes to an irresistible creamy consistency balanced in acids and sugars, salsa is at its best. Tomato sauce is eaten all year round, and all Sicilian women will make enough salsa to last through the winter. I must say it is handy to have in storage. It is also handy if someone makes some for you.

Makes 1 litre/4 cups/1¾ pints tomato sauce.

3kg (6lb) very ripe tomatoes
1 medium onion finely chopped
3 tablespoons extra virgin olive oil
½ teaspoon sugar, optional
6 fresh basil leaves

Wash the tomatoes and bring to boil in a large stockpot with 4 cups of water until soft, about 10 minutes. Drain in a colander. Strain the tomatoes through a vegetable mill. Discard skin and seeds.

Warm the olive oil in a medium-sized saucepan (24cm/10in) and gently cook the onion until translucent. Add the tomatoes, bring to boil and reduce over medium heat for 5 to 7 minutes. Timing will depend on ripeness and amount of water in the tomatoes. Sauce must reach a light and creamy consistency. Season with salt and sugar if the sauce has a little acidity. Add the basil.

The tomato sauce can be kept in the fridge for up to one week or frozen in small plastic cups for later.

Fish and meat

Triglie di scoglio fritte
Fried red mullets

My grandfather Luigi excelled in frying fish. His frying always resulted in a perfectly gold-en hue and crunchy crust. I remember watching him adjust the flame to make sure the olive oil was always very hot but never burning and learned that good frying could be an art. Red rock mullets, *triglie di scoglio*, with their intensely red skin and small beard under the chin, have a varied diet which makes them tastier than fish that live on sandy shores.

Serves 4
 2 egg whites
 8 x 150g (4½oz) fresh red mullets or any firm fish
 1½ cups semolina flour
 extra virgin olive oil
 sea salt
 2 lemons cut in quarters, optional

Beat the egg whites and add a small pinch of salt. Wash the red mullet and pat dry with kitchen paper. Dip in the egg white, drip off excess egg and coat with the flour. Place on a wooden board.

Fill a deep frying pan with at least 4 cms (2½in) of olive oil and bring to frying temperature.

Shake off excess flour from the fish and drop in the sizzling olive oil, raising heat if it stops sizzling. Cook over high to medium high heat for 8 to 10 minutes depending on size, turning once. Fish is usually cooked when the eyes turn completely white and dry. Put on absorbent paper and sprinkle with sea salt just before serving.

Fry all fish this way. Serve immediately, with sliced lemon wedges.

Gamberi saltati in padella al marsala
Marsala sautéed prawns

The shores of Porto Palo are renowned for their small pink prawns or shrimps. A gentle dash of white wine or Marsala enhances their delicate flavour.

Serves 4
    4 tablespoons extra virgin olive oil
    2 cloves garlic
    a pinch of chilli
    1kg (2lb) small prawns (shrimps)
    marsala or white wine
    1 tablespoon flat leaf parsley, finely chopped

In a large pan, warm 4 tablespoons of olive oil with the garlic and chilli.

Add the prawns (shrimps) and sauté over medium heat until they begin to change colour—about 5 minutes depending on size. Season with a dash of salt, sprinkle with some marsala or wine, and let evaporate over high heat for a couple of minutes. Mix in the parsley and switch off. Serve warm.

Sarde alla brace
Grilled sardines

Menfi is a relatively young town in Sicily, dating back only to the 17th century, with few culinary traditions. There is one, however, and that is grilled sardines on the beach on the night of Ferragosto, August 15 —Italy's major holiday. In the months between June and September, this tasty fish is at its best: fat and ideal for grilling. We make *Sarde alla brace* at La Gurra at the beginning of September to celebrate the end of the grape harvest with the workers. It is a merry feast with singing, jokes and roars of laughter and it is a man's only event. Sardines are put on cane skewers and cooked on an open fire over vine wood. It is a custom to eat them with your hands by biting along the spine, with a raw onion on the side.

Serves 4
    2-3 large red or pink onions, thickly sliced
    1 tablespoon sea salt
    1 tablespoon vinegar
    15 sardines per person, gutted

Marinate the onion in a bowl with water and a tablespoon each of salt and vinegar for at least an hour. Drain before serving.

Place sardines on a flat cane skewer placed below the spine, on the side of the belly. Season with salt and cook over a wooden fire for 5 to 7 minutes per side.

Serve hot with raw onion on the side.

The fishmonger in Menfi cleaning sardines. In August they are fat and ideal for grilling.

Insalata di polipo e patate
Octopus and potato salad

The season for octopus starts early in spring and lasts throughout the summer. The best variety is *maiolino*—it is reddish brown and has two rows of suckers on its tentacles. When I returned to live in Sicily, I could not stop myself from having *Insalata di polipi,* which have to be very fresh to maintain their intense sea flavour. One evening some friends showed up for dinner unexpectedly and as I did not have enough *polipi* for all, I added potatoes and came up with this salad.

Serves 4

1 cup of white wine
1 small octopus, about 800g (1½lb)
1 celery stalk, coarsely chopped
10 olives in brine, rinsed, pitted and halved
freshly ground pepper
extra virgin olive oil
2 tablespoons flat parsley, finely chopped
400g (13oz) new potatoes, boiled, skinned and chopped in cubes

Bring a stockpot of salted water to boil. Add a cup of white wine. Hold the octopus from the head and dip the tentacles in and out of the water three times. Then drop the whole octopus in. Cover with a lid and cook over medium heat for 20 minutes from boiling point. Switch off, remove lid and leave in the water for a further 20 minutes. This will make it soft.

Remove the octopus from the water and cut the tentacles from the head. Chop thicker part of tentacles into smaller pieces, longer as they get thinner. The head is considered the connoisseurs' mouthful, the tastier part of the octopus, but not everyone likes it. In that case, empty it of its interior juices (ink) and add the outer part to the tentacles. Otherwise, add it whole to the salad.

In an oval or round serving dish, mix the octopus with the celery, olives and season with pepper, olive oil and parsley. Leave to infuse for at least an hour and add potatoes just before serving. Serve at room temperature.

Coniglio con la caponata
Rabbit with caponata

Because of their strong flavour, all wild rabbits used to be marinated in wine all night. I have tried this recipe with domestic rabbit as well and it is absolutely delicious.

Serves 6

  2kg (4lb) wild or domestic rabbit, cut in pieces
  ½ litre (16fl oz) red wine
  4 bay leaves
  1 twig fresh rosemary
  1½ cups extra virgin olive oil
  2 large onions, coarsely chopped
  2 large carrots, chopped
  2 celery stalks, chopped
  1 cup plain flour
  ¼ teaspoon cinnamon
  ¼ teaspoon cloves
  2 tablespoons red wine vinegar
  2 tablespoons sugar
  2 tablespoons lemon zest finely grated

Marinate the rabbit with the wine and herbs for at least three hours or overnight, turning at least once.

Warm the olive oil in a large skillet and cook the onion, celery and carrots over medium high heat until crispy but not burned. Remove to a side plate and retain oil in skillet. Shake off excess wine from rabbit pieces, coat with flour and sauté over a high heat in the skillet.

Move all cooked rabbit into a clean large pot, cover with the onion, celery and carrot mixture. Season with the cloves, cinnamon and some salt. Deglaze skillet with the wine marinade, pour this liquid over the rabbit, cover with about 300 ml (10 fl oz) warm water and cover over medium high heat for 1 to 1½ hours or until rabbit is soft.

Adjust salt and braise with the vinegar mixed with the sugar, until well evaporated. Add the lemon zest and switch off.

Leave to rest for the sweet and sour flavours to combine until ready to serve.

Desserts

Gelo di melone
Chilled watermelon pudding

This pudding carries traces of Arabic flavours. Traditionally, jasmine was left to macerate all night in a cup of water and then added to the juice during cooking.

Makes 8 x 120 ml bowls
  1.2 kg (2lb, 1oz) of watermelon pulp (about 2 kg (4lb) including skin) to
      make 1 litre (1¾ pints) watermelon juice
  70g (2oz) wheat starch
  200g (7oz) sugar
  8 jasmine flowers
  ⅓ cup unsweetened black chocolate, finely chopped
  1 tablespoon pistachio, chopped
  cinnamon powder

Cut watermelon in pieces and squeeze through a mouli or juicer.

In a medium-sized stockpot mix the wheat starch with the sugar. Strain the watermelon juice through a sieve and add gradually, stirring with a wooden spoon or whisk. Add all the juice and cook over a medium heat, stirring continuously to prevent sticking until it reaches boiling point—about 7 minutes. Switch off heat. The mixture will have a light creamy consistency and coat the back of the wooden spoon.

Pour into individual glass bowls or in a single glass bowl and allow to cool.

Sprinkle with the chocolate, pistachio and a dash of cinnamon. Top with a jasmin flower at the centre of the pudding and refrigerate. Serve cold. It can keep in the fridge for up to four days.

Next page: In the summer there is always a watermelon pudding ready to be eaten.

Gelatina di uva con mandorle tostate
White grape pudding with toasted almonds

My mother makes this white grape pudding towards the end of the summer in the brief period between mid-August to mid-September when grapes are at their sweetest. It is a refreshing, slightly pungent and rather unusual dessert.

Makes around 8 x 120 ml bowls

2kg (4lb) sweet white grapes to make 1 litre (1¾ pints) grape juice
70g (2oz) wheat starch
¼ cup white sugar, you may need more depending on sourness of grapes
½ teaspoon cinnamon powder
1 tablespoon chopped toasted pine nuts or chopped almonds

Wash grapes and separate fruit from stalks. Squeeze through a mouli or juicer and strain the juice through a sieve onto a bowl. Use juice straight away or refrigerate as it will start fermenting.

In a medium-sized stockpot, mix the sugar with the wheat starch and whisk in the grape juice. Slowly bring to boil over a medium high heat, stirring constantly. Switch off as soon as it reaches boiling temperature. It should be of a light creamy consistency.

Pour into individual glass bowls and allow to cool.

Sprinkle with a pinch of cinnamon and some toasted pine nuts or chopped almonds and refrigerate.

Serve cold. It can keep in the fridge for up to four days.

Pesche al vino bianco e menta
Peaches with white wine and mint

Notwithstanding their love affair with sweets, Sicilians eat relatively few cakes in the summer. Meals tend to finish with *Gelo di melone* (see page 97), ice-creams bought in the gelaterie, or fresh fruit. To end a more formal dinner, *Pesche al vino bianco e menta* is often served.

Serves 4

5 peaches, cut into quarters and then halved
¼ cup dry white wine
1 tablespoon sugar
½ teaspoon cinnamon
8 fresh mint leaves

Mix the peaches with the wine, sugar and cinnamon in a glass bowl and refrigerate for at least an hour. Add the mint leaves just before serving.

Fichi e guastella
Figs and guastella cheese

August is the month of sweet figs at La Gurra. We all have our own special trees around the farm and as ripening time approaches there is a continuous checking of which should be picked. Although both white and black figs are mouth watering, the general opinion is that only the black ones picked towards the end of August, are worth having. This is also the time of the year when shepherds make *guastella,* a delicate sheep's milk cheese from the Belice Valley which is now starting to get its due recognition.

Serves 6

12 green figs
6 slices of a mild sheep's milk cheese

Peel the figs and chill until ready to serve alongside slices of a mild sheep's milk cheese.

Right: *Pesche al vino bianco e menta.*

Parfait di mandorle
Almond parfait with a hot chocolate sauce

Palermo's ice-creams are some of the world's best: its coffee flavour is unrivalled. Watermelon, mulberry, hazelnut or chocolate ice-creams are eaten in a warm bun topped with sweetened whipped cream for breakfast. This is one of the few homemade ice-creams.

Serves 6
  200g (7oz) almonds, peeled
  400g (14oz) sugar, plus 20g (½oz) to be added to the cream
  6 eggs
  1 litre (1½ pint) of cream
  200g (7oz) black chocolate or cocoa powder
  ¼ cup marsala or other liquor

Toast the almonds in a skillet with 200g (7oz) of the sugar over a low heat, stirring continuously until caramelised. Oil a marble surface or plastic board and pour the almond and sugar mixture over the surface, flattening it as much as possible with a kitchen spatula and leave to cool. When it is cold, break into crumbs and small pieces.

Separate the yolks from the egg whites. Beat the yolk in a bowl with 180g (6½oz) of the sugar until white and fluffy. In a food processor, beat the egg whites until stiff. Whisk the cream with 20g (½oz) of sugar.

Add the cream to the egg yolks and mix in the almonds. Now gradually add in the egg white, one spoonful at a time, mixing it from top to bottom until it is well blended. Wet a rectangular mould with a bit of water or line with baking paper, and pour in the cream. Place in the freezer for at least 24 hours.

When ready to serve, melt the chocolate and mix with the marsala. Alternatively, make a chocolate cream with black cocoa powder, and a teaspoon of milk and water or until it reaches a creamy consistency.

Turn out the ice cream and top with hot chocolate sauce.

Autumn

Autumn in Sicily is a time of exceptional beauty and the season we recommend for visiting the island. As the torrid heat disappears, it leaves crystalline blue skies and a crowdless sea to be enjoyed.

Often the only signs of autumn are the brightly coloured prickly pears, pomegranates and our little orchard of lotus fruits. Otherwise, warm weather stretches well into November with temperatures remaining around 25°C (77°F) until the warm spell suddenly 'breaks' and the rains finally move in.

Autumn is also one of the busiest times of the year on the farm. As the grape harvest finishes at the end of September, it leads straight into the picking of table olives at Belicello. Within the first ten days of October, depending on how hot the summer has been, the main olive harvest begins with the picking of the early varieties of oil olives at La Gurra.

The olive harvest is a labour-intensive time of the year that can last up to ten weeks, taking us into the wetter months of November and December. Days shorten and long evenings are spent at the press.

The only reward after a day's hard work is the intense flavour and taste of freshly pressed extra virgin olive oil poured straight out of the press over a large piece of warm bread, seasoned with oregano and sea salt.

At home, basic dishes like *Spaghetti con olio e parmigiano* or *Crema di fave* highlight its fragrance. Autumn is also marked by green cauliflower used in *Pasta con i broccoli in tegame* or squash, used in *Zucca in agrodolce*.

Fish is also back in the markets in great abundance and variety and we often drive down to Porto Palo in time to meet the boats. The Mediterranean sea is renowned for its saltiness and this probably adds to the intensity of flavour in Sicilian fish. You will rarely eat fish filleted as it is always cooked whole, either grilled, baked or fried, depending on the variety.

Linguine con la bottarga
Linguine with tuna roe

Dried tuna roe is produced in the province of Trapani where the tradition of tuna fishing is lost in time. The catching of the king of blue fish is still carried on today, in May, off the Egadi island of Favignana. Make sure the *bottarga* or roe you buy is still light pink in colour and moist, a sign of freshness. Otherwise, it will be salty.

Serves 4
    400g (12oz) linguine or pennette lisce
    4 garlic cloves
    ½ cup extra virgin olive oil
    a pinch of fresh or dried chillies
    100g (3½oz) tuna roe or bottarga, peeled and chopped in a food processor
    50g (1½oz) butter
    2 tablespoons flat parsley, finely chopped
    zest of a lemon, grated

Marinate the garlic and chillies in the olive oil for at least an hour, in a covered bowl to preserve fragrance of the olive oil.

In a medium-sized serving bowl, mix the butter with half the roe and the lemon zest.

Bring a large stockpot of salted water to boil. Cook the pasta according to package directions and drain, reserving ¼ cup of its cooking water.

Mix with the butter and fish roe until well combined. Remove garlic cloves and mix in the oil, the remaining roe and half the parsley. Adjust with a spoonful of pasta water if necessary.

Top with remaining parsley and serve immediately.

Penne con crema di olive Nocellara
Penne with nocellara olive paste

Nocellara olives are one of the most well-known green table varieties in Sicily. They originated in the Castelvetrano area and are also appreciated for their fragrant oil. Table olives are picked by hand and must be in perfect condition and at least 21mm in size or they are discarded and used for oil.

Serves 4

> 300g (10oz) nocellara or other green olives in brine, washed and pitted
> 1 garlic clove
> 4 anchovy fillets
> 4 sundried tomatoes
> ½ cup extra virgin olive oil
> 1 pinch of fresh or dried chillies
> 400g (12oz) penne pasta
> 2 tablespoons parsley, finely chopped

Blend the olives in a food processor with the garlic, anchovies, sundried tomatoes, extra virgin olive oil, and chillies until creamy. If making this in advance, store in a jar and top generously with extra virgin olive oil.

Bring a stockpot of salted water to boil and cook the pasta according to package directions. Drain and pour into a bowl.

Mix with the olive paste and half the parsley until well combined. Sprinkle with remaining parsley and serve.

Caserecce con i broccoli in tegame
Caserecce with saffron cauliflower, dried raisins and pine nuts

Stacks of light green cauliflowers, called *broccoli* in Sicily rather than *cavolfiore* as in the rest of Italy, are one of the most recurrent signs of autumn in market stalls. This pasta has deep Arabic influences with saffron, dried black raisins, pine nuts, and sometimes sundried tomato paste. I use anchovy fillets instead of *sarde salate* (salted sardines), as they are more delicate. Without the pasta, the vegetables make a good side dish for a roast or sausages.

Serves 4
- 1 medium-sized cauliflower, about 500g (1lb)
- ½ medium-sized onion, finely chopped
- 1 pinch fresh or dried chillies
- 20g (¾oz) dried black raisins
- 10g (½oz) pine nuts
- 4 anchovy fillets
- 1 teaspoon saffron stigmas
- 400g (12oz) bucatini or caserecce pasta
- 1 cup ragusano cheese, mild pecorino or parmesan cheese, freshly grated
- ¼ cup extra virgin olive oil

Cut the stalks from the cauliflower florets and chop into small pieces as they need to cook more than the florets.

Fill a medium-sized stockpot with water and bring to the boil. Add salt and the cauliflower stalks and boil for about five minutes before adding the florets. Cook until stalks soften—about ten minutes. Remove the cauliflower with a slotted spoon into a separate bowl and reserve the water in the stockpot.

In a cup, cover the saffron stigmas with two spoonfuls of the hot cauliflower water. Warm five tablespoons of oil in a medium-sized skillet, add the onion, a small pinch of chilli and cook under slow heat until transparent. Add the dried black raisins and pine nuts, stir for a further 2 minutes and add the anchovy fillets. Add the cauliflower, saffron and two ladles of cauliflower water. Adjust salt and cook over medium heat until soft and mushy, about 7 minutes. The vegetables can be prepared a day in advance.

If cooking on the same day, add more water to the stockpot and bring to the boil. Cook pasta according to package directions and drain well.

Pour pasta back into the stockpot and mix with the cauliflower over medium heat for a couple of minutes. Pour into a large serving bowl, mix in the cheese and serve hot.

Spaghetti con olio nuovo e pecorino
Spaghetti with new season's extra virgin olive oil and pecorino

Although Giuseppe, my husband, doesn't cook, he makes his own pasta with extra virgin olive oil adding a couple of spoons of pasta water to thin it out. He has now introduced this very old Sicilian custom to our family. I use it to cream many pasta sauces, reducing the amount of fats often used. The use of fragrant freshly pressed olive oil makes it an exceptional dish.

Serves 4
    400g (12oz) spaghetti or pennette lisce
    ¾ cup of new season's extra virgin olive oil
    4 tablespoons mild pecorino or parmesan cheese, freshly grated
    freshly ground black pepper
    1 tablespoon parsley, finely chopped

Bring a stockpot of salted water to boil. Cook the pasta according to directions.

Whisk the olive oil with the cheese, a little pepper and half the parsley in a medium-sized serving bowl. Mix in about 3 tablespoons pasta water a few minutes before draining.

Drain the pasta, pour into the serving bowl and mix until well combined with the oil. Top with remaining parsley and serve immediately.

Arancine di riso con la béchamel
Orange shaped rice balls with a white sauce filling

Arancine (literally translated as 'small oranges') are one of the most popular street foods of Sicily. They come from the Arabic nomads, who ate the bulgur wheat balls as they travelled across the North African desert. They developed into a more elaborate rice version in Sicily. The Sicilian-Arab *arancina* has a meat filling cooked with tomato extract, cinnamon, pine nuts, sultanas and is round in shape. The *Arancina in bianco*, a result of French-influenced nineteenth century cuisine, is oval and has a cheese and béchamel filling. Thanks to *arancine*, some Sicilian chefs claim that the famous *Risotto alla Milanese* is nothing more than an unsuccessful *arancina*. Make a small quantity of meat sauce and try both versions and freeze them, ready for a cocktail party. You will not regret it.

Serves 6—makes 24 x 80g arancine
    500g (1lb) arborio or roma rice
    100g (3½oz) butter
    50g (1½oz) parmesan cheese, freshly grated
    1 teaspoon saffron powder
    salt

    For the béchamel sauce:
    25g (3/4oz) butter
    25g (3/4oz) plain flour
    250ml (8fl oz) milk
    40g (1½oz) mozzarella cheese, finely chopped
    50g (1¾oz) primosale or a mild cheese, finely chopped
    40g (1½oz) thick slice of cooked ham, finely chopped

    For the batter:
    2 cups plain flour
    3 cups breadcrumbs for coating
    extra virgin olive oil for frying

Cook the rice in 1½ litres (2½ pints) of salted boiling water according to package directions. Drain and spoon back into stockpot. Season with the butter, 6 tablespoons of parmesan and saffron until well combined. Leave the rice to cool as this will make it easier to bind. Rice can be made up to half a day in advance.

Make the béchamel sauce by melting the butter in a small casserole. Whisk in the flour over low heat for about 1 minute. Gradually add the warm milk, whisking constantly until blended. Raise heat and stir until it comes to the boil, cook for 1 minute and switch off. Season with salt and remaining parmesan. Once cold, add the cheeses and ham. The béchamel can also be made a day in advance.

Line all ingredients up in front of you on a flat surface: a small bowl with water for your hands, the rice, the béchamel mixture, a teaspoon and a board or dish to put the rice balls on.

Moisten the palm of your left hand with water and top with a thin, flattened layer of rice of about 7cms (2½ in). Top with 1½ teaspoons of béchamel and cover with a similar handful of rice. Pat together, shaping into an oval 7 x 5cm (2½ x 2in) ball. If any of the béchamel 'leaks' it helps the rice to stick. The filling is the tastier part, so make sure there is plenty of it. Place on a dish ready to refrigerate. Make all the *arancine* this way.

The *arancine* can be fried straight away or left in the fridge until the next day. This helps the rice stick further. They can also be frozen at this point. (When defrosting, bring the rice balls to room temperature before coating in the batter and breadcrumbs and frying.)

When ready to cook the *arancine*, make a thin batter in a bowl by whisking the flour with the water and a pinch of salt until smooth. Pour breadcrumbs into another large dish for coating.

Pat *arancine* again into shape, dip into the batter, shake off excess batter and roll into the breadcrumbs patting further to make sure *arancine* are compact and the coating even and smooth.

In a deep frying pan, bring the oil to frying temperature and fry the *arancine* over medium heat until golden, turning regularly as they cook. Place on absorbent paper and serve warm.

Timballo di pasta con le sarde
Sardine, wild fennel and pasta timbale

Serves 6

400g (12oz) wild fennel shoots,
  cleaned
1 tablespoon extra virgin olive oil
1 medium-sized onion, finely
  chopped
25g (1oz) dried black currants,
  soaked in warm water
25g (1oz) pine nuts
¼ tablespoon saffron

600g (1¼lb) fresh sardines, filleted
½ cup dry white wine
400g (12oz) pasta, bucatini or
  penne lisce
1 tablespoon tomato paste
½ cup breadcrumbs
15g (½oz) almonds chopped
17–18 anchovy or sardine fillets
  in oil

Boil the wild fennel shoots in a stockpot of salted water, until stems are soft—about 15 minutes. Drain, reserving the water for later use and chop finely.

Warm the olive oil in a large skillet and cook the onion until translucent. Add the currants, pine nuts, saffron and anchovy fillets and stir the mixture together. Mix in the sardine fillets, pour the wine over the mixture and cook for another 3 minutes, stirring gently over medium heat. Dissolve the tomato paste in ½ cup of warm water, add to the mixture, adjust salt, cook for a further minute and switch off.

Preheat oven to 200°C (400°F) Gas Mark 5.

Coat a 20cm (8in) tin at least 8cm (3in) high with oil. Shake breadcrumbs up to the sides.

Add a bit more water to the fennel water in the stockpot, bring it back to a boil, adjust salt and cook the pasta. Drain three minutes before suggested time, reserving some fennel water, and pour pasta back into the stockpot. Season with the chopped wild fennel, half a cup extra virgin olive oil and half the sardine mixture.

The pasta sauce should be thin as it tends to dry in the oven. Add a ladleful or two of fennel water if necessary. Lay an even layer of plain sardines on the bottom of the tin and cover with a layer of pasta. Cover the pasta with the sardine mixture and top with pasta. Sprinkle with remaining breadcrumbs and chopped almonds.

Place in the oven and cook for about 35 minutes or until it forms a light crust on the top. Cool for about 20 minutes and mould onto a serving dish. Serve at room temperature. This dish improves as it rests, even for a whole day.

Made into a *timballo*, *Pasta con le sarde*, becomes more appropriate for a dinner or a buffet. This was a tradition in my mother's family and my mother (right) still makes it.

Vegetables

Zucca in agrodolce con la menta
Sweet and sour pumpkin with mint

Sweet and sour flavours, combined with the mildness of pumpkin, are given a little punch by the chillies and garlic in this staple dish. I serve it with *Involtini di carne* or *Sarde a Beccafico* or as one of many starters for a buffet. It is best made a day in advance.

Serves 4

500g (1lb) pumpkin, cut into thick slices
3 tablespoons extra virgin olive oil
2 garlic cloves, cut into slivers
a pinch of fresh or dried chillies
sea salt
½ cup red wine vinegar
2 teaspoons sugar
6 mint leaves

Warm the olive oil and add the garlic and chillies over a low heat for a couple of minutes without burning. Add the pumpkin, season with salt, mix, cover with a lid and cook until tender—about 8 minutes. Add a bit of water during cooking if necessary.

When almost ready, mix the vinegar with the sugar in a cup. Increase heat and pour over the pumpkin. Reduce for a couple of minutes, adjust salt and switch off. Place on a serving dish and leave to cool until needed. Top with mint leaves before serving.

With over 400 years of Spanish history, the use of sweet and sour is well entrenched in Sicilian cuisine.

Peperoni con crema di capperi e menta
Capsicums with capers and mint pâté

This is a colourful dish on a buffet table. It can be served both as a starter or alongside a second course. Substitute mint with parsley, depending on what is available.

Serves 4

5 large red and yellow capsicums (peppers)

For the pâtè:
½ cup extra virgin olive oil
3 anchovy fillets
½ cup capers in salt, thoroughly washed in water and milk
½ cup fresh mint or parsley
12 black olives in brine, pitted
1 small garlic clove
6 sundried tomatoes

Warm oven to 200°C (400°F) Gas Mark 5. Place (peppers) on oven rack and cook for 40 minutes, or until skin begins to wrinkle.

In the meantime, mix all ingredients for the pâté in an electric blender until creamy. The pâté can also be stored in the fridge in a glass jar topped with olive oil and used for canapés.

Remove peppers from the oven, place them in a bowl and cover with plastic wrap. The moisture released will make peeling easy. When cooler, peel off the skin, remove stem and all the seeds. Break up into strips or fillets and place in a colander to drain off excess liquids.

Line fillets next to each other in alternating colours in a round or oval ceramic dish. Spoon over the pâté and top with extra mint leaves or parsley and a bit more oil, if necessary.

Serve at room temperature.

Fish, meat and eggs

Sgombri panati
Breaded mackerel

This tasty blue fish is very common in Mediterranean waters. The lemon and wine in this recipe combine to enhance the mackerel's natural flavour. It is one of the varieties of fish loved by my son Alfredo.

Serves 4

    4 mackerels, about 250g (8oz) each, boned and filleted
    ½ cup extra virgin olive oil
    2 tablespoons parsley, finely chopped
    1½ cups breadcrumbs
    1 cup white wine
    1 freshly squeezed lemon
    1 lemon cut into wedges

Place the fish fillets in a large dish, coat with olive oil and parsley and marinate for up to an hour.

Warm oven to 180°C (350°F) Gas Mark 4.

Pad the fish fillets with the breadcrumbs and place in a greased ovenproof dish or tray. Top with white wine, lemon juice, a dash of salt and cook for about 10 minutes. Alternatively, cook the fillets on a non stick pan, turning them once until cooked and golden, about 5 minutes.

Serve warm with lemon wedges on the side.

Sarde a beccafico
Rolled sardines with pine nuts and raisins

I have become addicted to *Sarde a beccafico*. This dish is made when the sardines are fat and tender, either in spring or autumn. Sicilian fishmongers prepare them by scaling them and removing the head and backbone. Leave the two fillets attached and the tail on for decoration.

Serves 4

    1kg (2lb) of sardines, head and backbone removed, yields 600g (1¼lb)
    100g (4oz) breadcrumbs
    20g (¾oz) pine nuts
    20g (¾oz) dried black currants
    ½ cup extra virgin olive oil
    2 tablespoons orange juice
    zest of one orange, finely shredded
    2 tablespoons parsley, finely chopped
    1 teaspoon of sugar
    1 pinch of salt
    15 bay leaves
    ¼ cup dry white wine
    2 tablespoons lemon or orange juice

Wash the sardines and pat dry.

Warm oven to 180°C (350°F) Gas Mark 4.

In a bowl, mix the breadcrumbs with the pine nuts, currants, olive oil, orange juice and zest, parsley, sugar and a pinch of salt.

Grease an oven serving dish about 18 x 30 cm (7in x 30in) with a teaspoon of olive oil. Roll each sardine around a teaspoon of the breadcrumb mixture (or as much as they will take) starting from the head end and leaving the tail to close it off. Place sardines tightly next to one another to prevent them opening up. Insert a piece of bay leaf in between two rolls. Do all sardines this way and top with any remaining bread-crumb mixture.

Sprinkle with a bit of wine and cook for 10 minutes.

Remove from the oven, top with lemon or orange juice.

Serve warm or at room temperature.

Sarde allinguate
Fried sardines dipped in vinegar

Children love these, and they also make an excellent starter alongside a cold glass of white wine.

Serves 4
  20 medium-sized sardines, about 400g (¾lb)
  ½ cup white wine vinegar
  1 cup semolina flour
  extra virgin olive oil for frying
  salt

Ask your fishmonger to scale the sardines and open into fillets or clean them yourself by removing the head and running your fingers down alongside the belly of the fish and removing the gills and stomach. As the fish opens, lift the backbone and remove, by breaking it off at the tail end, leaving the two fillets attached. Cut off the small dorsal fin, especially if serving to children. Rinse and leave on a colander over a plate until excess water has dripped off or dry on paper towel.

Place sardine fillets in a bowl, cover with the vinegar, season with a pinch of salt and marinate for up to an hour. Drain, shake off excess vinegar and coat with the flour.

In a deep frying pan, warm the extra virgin olive oil to frying temperature.

Shake off excess flour and dip sardines, a few at a time so they do not overlap, into the hot oil. Fry over medium high heat until golden—about two minutes.

Dry on paper towel, sprinkle with a dash of salt.

Serve warm or at room temperature.

Sogliola al vino bianco e capperi
Sole cooked in white wine with capers

One of my early childhood memories is eating sole from the sandy shores of the spa and fishing town of Sciacca. When we came to Menfi, one of my grandfather's main concerns was that I would eat good fresh fish. We would leave the house at around five in the afternoon, after my grandfather's nap, and drive along the tortuous road to Sciacca for the arrival of the day's catch. The fishmonger was in the centre of town, which is unusually divided into three sectors: the fishermen's, the nobility's and the farmers'. Great care was taken by my grandfather to choose the perfect sole. He cooked it himself, with *Patate a spezzatino* on the side. I add the smallest and mildest capers I can get from the farm.

Serves 4
    2 x 800g (1½lb) sole, scaled
    1 cup plain flour
    50g (1½oz) butter
    ½ cup extra virgin olive oil
    1 cup dry white wine
    salt
    2 tablespoons flat parsley, finely chopped
    3 tablespoons small capers in brine, desalted in water and milk

Dry the sole with paper towel and coat with flour.

In a large pan where you can fit both fish, warm the butter with the olive oil and add the soles skin side up. Add 1½ cups of water and the wine, cover with a lid and cook over medium heat for about 10 minutes. Remove lid, season with salt and simmer for a further 3 minutes or until cooked. Top with the capers, parsley and remove from heat.

Reduce juices further if needed and pour over the fish.

Serve immediately.

Dentice al forno
Baked dentex

Fish abound during the *bonaccia di ottobre*—the calm waters of October—before winter settles in. Fish is generally served whole and always cut at the table in front of you. The mouthfuls around the head, cheeks and small fillets are so delicious it would be a pity to miss them. This is how dentex, bream or bass are usually cooked.

Serves 4
  1.2kg (2½lb) dentex, bream or bass, scaled and gutted
  ¼ cup dry white wine
  1 cup extra virgin olive oil
  salt
  4 tablespoons parsley or oregano, finely chopped
  juice from one lemon, sieved

Warm oven to 180°C (350°F) Gas Mark 4.

Lightly grease a baking tray and place the fish on it. Sprinkle some salt in the stomach, pour over the wine and half a cup of water. Bake until cooked—about 45 minutes. The fish is ready when the dorsal fin pulls off.

In the meantime, beat the extra virgin olive oil with the lemon juice and parsley or oregano in a saucer and keep ready to serve alongside the fish.

Place on a serving dish and serve with boiled potatoes on the side.

Autumn is an excellent time for fishing. Signor Tarantino (centre) and his family have supplied us with fish for generations.

Involtini di carne
Meat parcels

Serves 6—about 30 involtini

½ cup of onion, finely chopped
½ cup chopped tomato
200g (7oz) white bread crumb
200g (7oz) ricotta infornata,
   parmesan or pecorino cheese,
   freshly grated
2 tablespoons pine nuts
2 tablespoons parsley, finely
   chopped
freshly ground pepper
salt

600g (1¼lb) veal rump steak slices,
   pounded and cut into 8 x 6 cm
   strips
10–15 bay leaves, cut in small strips
1 medium sweet onion, cut into
   wedges
finer breadcrumbs for coating, as
   needed
2 tablespoons dried black currants
extra virgin olive oil
skewers, soaked in water

Cook the onion with 3 tablespoons of oil and 3 tablespoons of water until soft. Add the chopped tomato, season with a pinch of salt and cook until soft.

Preheat oven to 200°C (400°F) Gas Mark 5.

Mix the breadcrumbs with the onion and tomato, cheese, sultanas and pine nuts in a medium-sized bowl. Season with pepper, salt and mix well. Filling must be compact yet moist.

Lay all the meat pieces on a flat surface and place a small ball of filling in the centre of each slice. Pull up the two sides and wrap the slice around the mixture to make a parcel. Fill all the slices this way.

Place about five rolls on each skewer, alternating a piece of bay leaf with a slice of onion every two pieces of meat.

Coat each skewer with oil, and pat with breadcrumbs.

You can cook these in the oven or in a non stick pan. Place on a greased tin and bake for about 25 minutes or until golden. Alternatively, grease a non stick pan with olive oil and cook meat parcels over medium heat, turning regularly until golden, about 10 minutes. Turn once.

Remove from the skewers and serve warm.

Landscape of La Gurra.

Uovo in tegamino con olio di oliva fresco
Shirred egg with new season's extra virgin olive oil

This is probably the first dish I cooked as a child in Menfi. We still used a *cucina economica*—a wood stove—that has now been replaced by modern gas stoves. In winter, the family used to gather around it, as it was such a wonderful source of heat. I remember starting to cook my own shirred egg in a small round pan with two handles, as grown ups were sipping glasses of red wine and slices of toasted bread dipped in fragrant new season's extra virgin olive oil. My main concern was to make sure the oil would not fry and retain its aromas. So, I mostly spooned the hot oil over the egg until it was cooked. My shirred eggs were an immediate success and for me, something new to play with.

   1 tablespoon new season extra virgin olive oil
   1 fresh farm egg
   1 pinch sea salt
   2 slices fresh bread

Pour the oil in a small stainless steel skillet and warm, about 5 seconds. Break in the egg sunny side up and cook by pouring over warm oil with a small spoon until ready, about three minutes. Remove from heat if the oil heats up or begins to sizzle. Season with a pinch of salt, top with more fresh extra virgin olive oil and serve warm with slices of fresh bread.

Spatola in agrodolce
Sweet and sour fish

Spatola or belt fish is an ugly, flat and silvery fish often over a metre long, which has been thought of as second rate until a few years ago. However, it is very delicate and has the advantage that it can be easily filleted. It has now grown in popularity all over Sicily but credit for introducing it to the menu should be given to Vittorio in Porto Palo, one the best fish restaurants in western Sicily. Even though his version has no equals, we have developed our own.

Serves 4

800g (1¾ lb) belt fish (or any firm, mild fish), filleted
1½ cups plain flour
extra virgin olive oil
400g (1lb) onions, thickly sliced
½ cup red wine vinegar
1 tablespoon sugar
½ cup small capers, rinsed in water and milk
mint leaves

Warm ½ cup of the olive oil in a medium-sized pan and cook the onions over medium–high heat until soft—about ten minutes. Add ½ cup of water if necessary. Mix the vinegar with the sugar and pour over the onions. Stir over high heat for another 3-5 minutes until vinegar has evaporated.

Pat dry the fish fillets and coat with flour. Warm the olive oil in a medium-sized pan and gently fry the fish over medium heat. Place on paper towel.

Place fish on a serving dish, top with the onions and garnish with mint leaves and capers.

Serve warm or at room temperature.

Desserts

Cotognata
Quince jelly

At the beginning of October, my mother has the quince apples from the trees across from the farmhouse picked to make quince jelly, which is put into terracotta moulds and left to dry in the cooling autumn sun on the balcony of the yellow living room. They absorb all the colours of explosive autumn sunsets before my mother puts them in for the night. The moulds represent religious themes such as the Madonna and Child, or animals, such as fish or sheep and have been in the house since I can ever remember. We have *cotognata* at the end of a meal, as a digestive with a glass of marsala or passito wine.

> 2 kg (4lb) quince apples
> 650g (1½lb) sugar per kilo (2lb) of pulp

Cut apples in quarters, skin on and remove pips.

Cook in a large saucepan over medium heat with a little bit of water until apples are soft. Dry any water in excess.

Weigh pulp and add 650g (1½lb) sugar for each kilogram. Put saucepan with apples and sugar back onto the stove and cook over medium heat stirring constantly, until water has dried completely—about ten minutes.

Strain the apple compote back into a stockpot and cook pulp over medium heat for a further ten minutes to dry out remaining water.

Pour into terracotta moulds and leave to dry in a ventilated area for at least a week. When it begins to feel dry remove from the moulds and leave to dry in a ventilated cupboard until needed.

Cotognata keeps well into the winter months.

Alongside a glass of passito, a slice of *Cotognata* ends a meal. Until it lasts…

Il segreto della dama
Ladies' secret dessert

The name of this dish is intriguing and lost in history. As children we loved the crunchiness and chocolate taste of this dessert that my grandmother, Natalia, regularly made. Today I make it for Alfredo's birthday parties or cut it into small squares and serve it with coffee. It is always a favourite and everyone asks for the recipe.

100g (3½oz) almonds, peeled
100g (3½oz) hazelnuts
100g (3½oz) plain tea biscuits
125g (4oz) butter, at room temperature
1 egg
25g (¾oz) bitter cocoa
175g (5½oz) sugar
a bit of icing sugar or extra almonds or walnuts for final decoration

Warm oven to 180°C (356°F) Gas Mark 4 and toast the almonds until golden.

In a food processor, blend the almonds with the hazelnuts and the biscuits into fine crumbs. Add the butter and egg, cocoa and sugar, mix and pour onto a flat surface. Blend all ingredients together by hand, breaking up any larger crumbs. Shape into a thin loaf, or any shape of your liking. Wrap in plastic film and store in the fridge for at least 24 hours.

Before serving, unwrap and decorate either with extra almonds or hazelnuts or simply with icing sugar. Cut into slices and arrange onto a serving dish.

Torta di cioccolato e mandorle
Almond and chocolate cake

This almond and chocolate cake is easy to make, has no flour and disappears as soon as it is cut.

Serves 4
    100g (7oz) dark cocoa powder
    200g (7oz) dark chocolate, softened
    300g (9oz) peeled almonds
    250g (8oz) of butter
    250g of sugar
    5 eggs
    1 sachet of vanilla powder
    icing sugar

Warm oven to 160°C (325°F) Gas Mark 3.

In a food processor, blend the chocolate and cocoa with the almonds into a fine paste. Pour into a bowl.

In the same blender, cream the butter and the sugar for 5 minutes until light and fluffy. Add one egg at a time and mix in the chocolate almond mixture until well combined.

Coat a 24cm (9in) pie dish with butter and flour, shaking off any excess flour or line with baking paper. Fill with the chocolate mixture.

Bake for 45 minutes. Turn onto a serving dish, cool and sprinkle with icing sugar before serving.

Next page: A dish for for chocolate lovers. I think anyone who has stayed with us more than one night has had a slice of *Torta di cioccolato e mandorle*.

Cuccia

Cuccia

Wheat is almost a synonym for *cuccia*, a dessert made on 13 December to thank Saint Lucia for having saved Sicily from a great famine with a ship full of it. As the population was starving they did not wait to grind it into flour and just boiled it. Over the years, it has been improved on and, because of the Sicilians' sweet tooth, turned into a dessert. It can be mixed either with a cream of ricotta or a simple white cream. Preparations for this dish start three days before.

200g (7oz) wheat
500g (1lb) ricotta, well drained
200g (7oz) sugar
100g (3½oz) black chocolate, finely chopped
cinnamon for topping

White cream:
½ litre (¾ pint) of milk
40g (1½oz) wheat starch
60g (2oz) sugar
rind of one lemon

Soak the wheat in plenty of water for three days, changing it every 12 hours. Drain the wheat and cook in plenty of slightly salted water until grains are soft—about 2 hours. Drain well.

In the meantime, prepare the ricotta cream as for the *Cannoli* filling (see page 57). Alternatively, make a white cream as in *Crema gialla* but omitting the eggs (see page 58).

Once the wheat is cold, mix with either of the creams and the chopped chocolate. Serve in a glass bowl topped with chocolate and cinnamon.

Nucatoli
Christmas biscuits

After Saint Lucia on 13 December, women in Menfi get together to make *nucatoli*, biscuits with an almond and honey filling. This marks the beginning of the Christmas festivities. They make up to 7 kilos at a time as *nucatoli* were offered as gifts to neighbours and family. As trays arrived at our house almost on daily basis, there was a continuous judging as to who made the best ones. The Mistretta family, who have lived in the next courtyard for generations, never failed to produce the best *nucatoli*. I asked the Mistretta cousins, Anna and Anna Maria (see page 148), for their *nucatoli* recipe for this book.

Ikg (2lb) white plain flour
300g (9oz) lard, at room temperature
300g (9oz) sugar
5g (⅙oz) sodium bicarbonate

Filling:
150g (5oz) almonds with their skin
125g (4oz) honey
dash of cinnamon

Glazing:
1 egg white
150g (5oz) icing sugar
1 teaspoon lemon juice
1 tablespoon pistachios, finely chopped
cinnamon powder

Mix the flour with the sugar, lard and sodium bicarbonate until the dough is soft and holds together. Put aside to rest overnight or a minimum of two hours.

Warm oven to 180°C (350°F) Gas Mark 4 and toast the almonds for 5 minutes. Grind in a food processor.

In a small pot, warm half a cup of water with the honey and bring to boil. Add the almonds and stir over medium heat until the paste comes off the sides of the pot. Make sure filling is dry or it will leak during the cooking of the biscuits. Switch off heat, pour into a glass bowl and leave to cool.

Roll the dough into 3 cm (1¾in) wide ropes and cut each one into ½ cm (¼in) slices. Flatten each slice with a rolling pin and fill with a ¼ teaspoon of the almond filling. Fold pastry around filling and give it an oval shape. The pastry is then carefully cut into thin wedges to produce a decoration which some people say resembles a dog with eight legs. Place biscuits on a tin covered with a sheet of baking paper and put in the oven. Cook for 12 minutes. If still white, grill for two minutes. Biscuits should be light golden in colour.

To make the glaze, mix the egg white with icing sugar in a mixer with a paddle over low speed. Traditionally it was combined softly and slowly with a pestle for at least fifteen minutes until it became thick and sticky when held between two fingers. Apparently, it took up to half a day to achieve the perfectly shiny glaze. We made it in a few minutes with excellent results.

With a thin brush, or your finger tip, lay a light coating of glaze over each biscuit. When dry, sprinkle with a dash of cinnamon and top with one pistachio.

Leave to cool and store in a tin.

Left: The glaze must remain while whilst the biscuits turn golden.
Right: Making the perfect glaze was an art that could take up to half a day.
Next page: Anna Mistretta and her cousin Anna Maria still make some of the best *nucatoli* in Menfi.

Winter

Activities at the farm are slowed only by the cold of December and Christmas. As the temperature drops, the house empties of guests and visitors. My father is the only one who survives bravely throughout the winter months in a house warmed only by fireplaces and glasses of hearty red wine. When the rest of us visit, we crowd around the fireplace waiting for the sky to come ablaze as the sun plunges beyond the Temples of Selinunte into the Mediterranean Sea.

Winter crops, however, yield a lot of the most delicious wild vegetables such as borage and beets, fennel and artichoke together with great quantities of lemons, tangerines and oranges of all varieties. As we gather indoors, more time is dedicated to cooking earthy dishes such as *Ragu di maiale*, that simmers for up to two days in a clay pot on a wooden stove, the ever present *Salsiccia in padella* with wild vegetables and artichokes made in a great variety of ways.

At the farm, winter seems only a whim of the elements. The lemon orchards with their golden fruits are in full production and the scent of lemon flowers, *zagara*, fills the air. It is blooming time also for almond trees, which, with their white or pink flowers, bring the first signs of spring as early as January.

Above: Moon rising over Menfi countryside early in March.

Below: Delicious wild vegetables grow in the *cavotto*, a magical spot with ancient oak and olive trees.

Pasta, rice and soup

Minestra di fave secche e verdura
Dried broad bean soup with wild vegetables

Not long ago, we invited a high-ranking politician over to dinner. For the occasion, he came with a following that included half his family, his brothers, his father ... Their farming origins breathed through their jackets and ties, but we made a point of showing them the *Minestra di fave–u maccu–* topped with fragrant fresh olive oil, which we served as a great delicacy. Associated with great poverty, this is a soup that would have never appeared on the tables of the upper classes. Recently, Sicilian chefs have also rediscovered dry *fave*, a dish of Roman origins. To us, it remains one of the best ways to taste fresh olive oil. Use a clay pot, if you have one, it will help maintain that slow simmering temperature, ideal for the success of this hearty soup.

Serves 4

300g (9oz) dried broad beans
½ onion, finely chopped
a small bunch of green leaves such as spinach, chicory
    or wild fennel shoots, optional
100g (3½oz) of pasta, ditalini or chopped spaghetti, optional
freshly ground black pepper
extra virgin olive oil, preferably new season
sea salt

In a bowl of cold water, soak the dried broad beans overnight (some varieties do not require soaking).

In a clay pot, sweat the onion in four tablespoons of olive oil until transparent. If adding wild fennel shoots, finely chop the stems and some of the finer shoots and cook with the onion. Drain and wash the beans in cold water. Add to the pot, stir for a couple of minutes and cover with 2 litres of cold water. Bring to the boil, lower heat, cover and simmer for about 2 hours, stirring occasionally until beans are soft and creamy. Add the salt halfway through cooking time. If the soup is too thick, add a bit of hot water.

If adding greens, chop them finely and combine with the soup for about twenty minutes before switching off.

In a small stockpot, cook the pasta and drain 2 to 3 minutes ahead of time. Add to the soup and cook for another 2 minutes with 3 tablespoons of olive oil before switching off.

Serve topped with new season olive oil and freshly ground pepper if the oil is not peppery enough.

Broad bean soup must cook slowly until beans become creamy. New season olive oil gives it the ultimate touch.

There is a special pleasure in eating wild vegetables. In winter, wild borage covers the fields of the *cavotto*, a magical spot with ancient oak and olive trees. We love drinking a cup of borage broth, renowned for its therapeutic properties (it is used for coughs and bronchitis), or eating it boiled with a drop of olive oil. One evening a friend dropped in unexpectedly for dinner. All I had was bundles of borage and couldn't think what on earth to cook. So, I put some borage on to boil and made this pasta which now appears regularly on his restaurant menu.

Serves 4

Bring water to boil in a medium-sized stockpot. Add the borage, a bit of salt and cook until the stems are tender, about five minutes. Scoop the borage into a bowl, retaining the water, and finely chop it with a knife.

Warm 4 tablespoons of olive oil in a medium-sized pan and cook the onion with two spoonfuls of borage water until soft, about 5 minutes. Throw in the borage and sauté over medium heat for about three minutes.

Add more water to stockpot and bring to the boil. Drop in the pasta, adjust the salt and cook until *al dente* according to package directions and drain.

Mix the pasta with the borage in a serving bowl, blend in the ricotta if using, a couple of spoonfuls of grated cheese and a drizzle more olive oil if necessary. Mix well and serve immediately.

This is a simple seasoning that allows the great flavour of the *spinelli* artichoke variety to infuse the pasta. *Spinelli* are medium-sized, very tasty artichokes, with spikes on the tip of the leaves. Choose them firm and without blemishes and do not discard the stems, just peel them and add to the sauce.

Serves 4

2 lemons
4 artichokes
½ cup extra virgin olive oil
2 tablespoons parsley, finely chopped
4 garlic cloves, whole
pinch of chilli, or 2 dried
400 g of short cut pasta, fusilli or similar
salt, to taste, plus extra for pasta water

Fill a medium-sized bowl with water, the juice of two lemons and the lemon halves. Cut the stalks off the artichoke, peel and chop finely. Tear off at least the first three rounds of leaves, breaking them off where they are tender. Now chop off the top half. Discard spiny ends. With a pair of scissors, cut off any spines or beard in the heart of the artichoke. Wipe extensively with the lemon and slice into thin wedges. Cover with the water and lemon solution. Prepare all artichokes this way.

Warm ¼ cup olive oil in a saucepan and gently simmer the garlic cloves with the chilli until soft. Add the artichoke stems and cook for a couple of minutes with a spoonful of water. Drain the wedges, remove any lemon seeds and toss with the oil over medium heat for a couple more minutes. Gradually add half a cup of water and cook gently for about ten minutes. Season with the salt, add remaining olive oil, half the chopped parsley and switch off.

Bring a stockpot of water to boil, add the salt, cook the pasta until *al dente* according to package directions and drain. Pour back into the saucepan and quickly stir with the artichokes over high heat for a minute or two. Pour onto a serving dish and sprinkle the remaining parsley on top. Serve with parmesan cheese on the side.

La Gurra's lemon groves tinge the countryside with a golden hue. Lemon trees produce fruit three times a year in an almost continuous cycle. The main winter harvest, *primo fiore* (first flower) produces the sweetest and most intensely scented fruits. After picking, the powerful scent of *zagara* fills the air as the plants prepare for the May harvest which produces *maiolini*—named after the month in which they are picked. July's crop, *verdello*, remains green but never reaches the market in its original colour. This pasta combines the fragrance of two of our best produce.

Serves 4

1 lemon, organic
½ cups extra virgin olive oil, new season if available
400g (12oz) of linguine, spaghetti or pennette lisce
⅓ cup parmesan cheese, freshly grated
freshly ground black pepper
parsley, finely chopped

Zest a lemon with a zester or vegetable peeler, avoiding the bitter white pith, and cut into fine shreds. Reserve a spoonful for final topping.

Marinate the lemon zest in half of the olive oil, in a medium-sized serving bowl covered with plastic wrap for up to an hour, if you have the time.

Bring a large stockpot of salted water to boil. Cook the pasta until *al dente* according to package directions.

In the meantime, add the remaining oil and whisk with the cheese, a bit of pepper, some of the parsley and three spoonfuls of cooking water.

Drain the pasta, pour into a serving bowl, and mix thoroughly with the oil and lemon zest until well combined. If needed, add a spoonful of pasta water to dilute sauce to a creamy consistency. Sprinkle with remaining parsley and lemon zest and serve immediately with more parmesan on the side.

Pasta must be mixed well with the seasoning in a bowl of adequate size to prevent it from sticking.

Wild asparagus has the most agreeable dash of bitterness. At La Gurra they grow mostly under the roots of the old olive trees and the lemon trees. They are rare, difficult to spot and it always seems someone else has got there before you. Delicious with either pasta or rice, we always reserve a few to add, boiled, to an egg gently fried in new season's olive oil. If using domestic asparagus, cook the stems separately from the tips and blend them to make a cream.

Serves 4

Remove hard ends from the asparagus and chop remaining stalk into small pieces. Reserve tips. Sweat the onion in 4 tablespoons of olive oil until transparent, add the stalks and cook with just under a cup of water until soft. Pour into a blender or food processor and coarsely chop. Pour everything back into pan, add the tips, season with the salt and saffron and cook gently for another 5 minutes or until stems are soft. Mix in the olive oil and switch off.

In the meantime, bring a stockpot of salted water to boil, cook the pasta until *al dente* according to package instructions and drain. Toss with the asparagus over high heat for 1 to 2 minutes. If needed, adjust thickness of sauce with some olive oil or pasta water.

Serve hot with parmesan cheese on the side.

The fennel seeds give this pork sauce a distinctive flavour. Sometimes a few sprigs of fennel shoots are also added but if you can't get wild fennel, substitute with rosemary or sage. Use a short, full-bodied pasta such as *rigatoni* or *casarecce* to contrast with the chunkiness of the sausage.

Serves 4

extra virgin olive oil
1 medium-sized onion, finely chopped
1 piece of celery stalk, finely chopped
1 medium carrot, coarsely chopped
a pinch of chilli, optional
600g (1¼lb) pork sausage meat
1 teaspoon wild fennel seeds or, alternatively, rosemary or sage
½ cup white wine
1–2 cups vegetable stock, if available
½ tablespoon tomato paste or ½ cup chopped tomatoes
400g (12oz) rigatoni or other medium-sized pasta
1 cup parmesan or pecorino cheese, grated

Warm ¼ cup of olive oil in a medium-sized sauce pan, add the onion, celery, carrot, and pinch of chilli and cook over medium to low heat for about five minutes. Add two spoonfuls of water or broth to prevent from browning.

Remove the meat from the casings and add to the vegetables with the fennel seeds. Increase heat and sauté the meat for five to seven minutes until it just begins to turn white, breaking it up with a wooden spoon. Pour in the wine and scrape the bottom of the pan of any juices. Season with pepper, add 1 cup of vegetable stock and simmer for a further ten minutes until meat is cooked.

In the meantime, dissolve the tomato paste in ½ cup of broth and stir into the meat. Alternatively, add the chopped tomatoes and cook with the meat. Just before switching off, mix in a couple of tablespoons of olive oil.

Bring a stockpot of water to boil, add the salt, cook the pasta and drain. Pour pasta back into stockpot, stir over a high heat with the sausage mixture, a drizzle of oil and half the cheese. Switch off and serve with more cheese on the side.

Salvino holds a bunch of wild fennel. The shoots start as early as November and last throughout winter and early spring.

A *fritto misto* is usually served on special occasions. Everything is coated in beaten egg, breadcrumbs and fried. You can also use the batter for *Arancine* (see page 115).

Makes 12

In a bowl or food processor, mix the flour and salt with the butter, adding the wine until it binds together. Knead for 2 to 3 minutes on a floured surface until you have a firm, yet elastic dough. Shape into a ball, wrap with cling film and leave to rest in a cool place for at least half an hour.

If the ricotta is fresh, leave to drip overnight in a colander or the filling will leak.

With a knife, or in a food processor, finely chop the salami. Pour the ricotta in a bowl and blend in the salami, cheese and freshly ground pepper with a fork, until well combined.

Roll the dough into a 5cm (2in) wide strip, cut off a slice and roll into a strip of about 10 x 3cm (4 x 1¾in). Add about half a spoon of the filling and fold the pastry around it, sealing the edges tightly to form a parcel. Fill all the pastry this way.

Heat the oil to frying temperature in a wide deep pan and fry the *panserotti* over medium heat until golden. Drain on paper towels and serve warm.

Right: *Panserotti* in the making. Next page: *Panserotti* ready to eat.

Crostini

Crostini are made of stale bread topped with primosale or any other mild cheese. Your children will love them and you may become an enthusiast too.

Serves 4

8 slices, two-day old bread
1 cup milk
1 egg
1 cup breadcrumbs
¼ litre (½ pint) dense béchamel sauce (see Crocchè di latte, page 170)
8 slices emmenthal or caciocavallo cheese
extra virgin olive oil for frying

Cut the bread into 2cm (¾in) slices and remove the crust. Pour about a cup of milk in a plate.

In a bowl, beat an egg with a pinch of salt. Fill a large plate or tray with breadcrumbs. Dip bread slices into the milk. Place a slice of cheese on the bread, top with a coating of white sauce patting it tightly on the bread. Dip into the egg and then coat with breadcrumbs. Prepare all slices this way and pat each one tightly.

Heat the oil in a deep frying pan and carefully drop in the *crostini*. Deep fry over medium to low heat, turning once until golden. Drain on paper towels and serve warm.

All the steps before frying can be made up to a day in advance and stored in the fridge. Bring back to room temperature for at least 1 hour before frying.

Have these once and you will end up keeping a little extra white sauce ready in your fridge for that last minute appetiser. *Crostini* and *Uova alla monacale* are usually made with leftover white sauce from this recipe so it's a good idea to make double the quantity.

Makes about 25

Melt the butter in a saucepan and stir in the flour over low heat. In the meantime, warm the milk then gradually whisk it into the roux. Season the sauce with salt, stirring constantly with a wooden spoon until it reaches boiling point and switch off. Remove from heat, mix in the parmesan and a shaving of nutmeg and leave to cool at least overnight as the sauce must be firm.

In a bowl, beat an egg with a pinch of salt.

Spread a large plate or tray with breadcrumbs.

Mould white sauce into dumplings, about half a tablespoon in size.

Dip into the beaten egg, remove with the help of a spoon and a fork, drip off excess egg and coat evenly with breadcrumbs. Make all dumplings this way, place them on a plate or tray and leave to rest or chill in the refrigerator for about 1 hour before frying.

Heat the oil in a pan and deep fry the *crocchè di latte* over medium to low heat until golden. Drain on paper towels and serve warm.

I don't know whether these eggs were made by nuns but they were never to be missed from my grandmother's *fritto misto*. Here eggs are hard boiled, the yolks mixed with a bit of béchamel and put back into the egg before being coated with breadcrumbs and fried. Today, Maria holds the secret of this recipe.

Serves 4

4 eggs, hard boiled
1 egg, beaten
1 tablespoon béchamel sauce (*besciamella di base*, page 148)
1 cup flour
1 cup breadcrumbs
extra virgin olive oil for frying

Cook the eggs in a small pot of boiling water for 8 to 10 minutes. Drain and cool with cold water. In a bowl, beat an egg with a pinch of salt.

Fill a large plate or tray with breadcrumbs.

Peel and slice the eggs lengthwise in half. Remove the yolks and combine with about 1 teaspoon or more of bechamel sauce. Put yolk mixture back into the egg and shape. Dip in the egg and coat evenly with breadcrumbs. Prepare all eggs this way patting each one tightly.

Heat the oil in a deep frying pan and carefully drop in the eggs. Fry over medium to low heat, turning once until golden. Drain on paper towels and serve warm.

We used to enjoy the farm a lot more, taking long walks through the old olive grove, searching for wild vegetables after the rains. Now with the development of our olive oil business, that now is only a memory. Today we shyly ask Salvino, one of our most devoted farmers who looks after our vegetable garden, if he has any extra time to find some wild greens. He has the best knowledge of wild vegetables of all the workers on the estate. He brings back baskets full of borage, wild chicory, beet or wild asparagus depending on the season. We use them the same day, boiled, and topped with olive oil. In most cases, my husband and I reserve the water to drink or to cook pasta with.

Serves 4

Wash the vegetables well in running water. Bring a large stockpot of salted water to boil. We only add very little salt as the vegetables have their own flavour and need very little. Cook the vegetables over a high heat, for about ten minutes or until stems are soft, depending on the variety.

Remove greens from water with the help of a scooping spoon or fork and transfer to a serving dish. Serve warm with fresh olive oil on the side. If cooking borage, we usually save a cupful of the water to drink.

Insalata di finocchi, olive nere e arance
Fennel salad with black olives and oranges

A salad made up of sliced oranges seasoned with olive oil and black olives is a very old-fashioned Sicilian winter salad. As my grandfather was very fond of fennel, he always added some. It is a refreshing and perfect way to end a meal. Choose round bulbs and keep in cold water and salt once they are cut.

Serves 4
    1 large fennel, hard outer leaves removed
    2 oranges
    ¼ cup extra virgin olive oil
    sea salt
    black pepper
    oregano
    16 black olives

Cut the fennel in quarters and then lengthwise into thin slices.

Peel oranges, removing all bitter white pith. Cut into thick slices and then cut in halves.

Mix oranges and fennel in a serving bowl more or less in equal amounts. Season with the oil, salt, pepper, oregano and mix. Top with the black olives and serve.

Stuffed artichokes are an all-time favourite, both as a starter or as a second course after a dish of pasta. Test them for freshness by making sure they feel hard and show no blemishes.

Serves 4

Fill a medium-sized bowl with water, the juice of a lemon and the lemon halves. Cut the stalks off the artichokes, peel and chop finely. Remove all the tough outer leaves, breaking them off where they are tender. One tough artichoke leaf can ruin an otherwise perfect mouthful. Now chop off the top half of the artichokes. Discard spiny ends. With the help of a pair of scissors, cut off any spines or beard in the heart of the artichokes. Cover with the water and lemon solution. Prepare all artichoke this way.

In a separate bowl, mix all the dry ingredients with 2–4 tablespoons of the oil to obtain a moist filling.

Drain one artichoke at a time and widen it in the centre. Season with a tiny pinch of salt, a drop of oil and fill with 2–2½ teaspoons of the breadcrumb mixture, pressing lightly until even. Prepare all the artichokes this way and place, upright, in a medium-sized skillet with sloping sides. Add the stalks, drizzle some oil over the artichokes and on the bottom of the pan, add a cup of water, a pinch of salt for general seasoning and cook with a lid on until tender, about 20 minutes. Check with a skewer for readiness.

During cooking and before serving, drizzle the juices over the filling.

Serve warm or at room temperature.

Below from left to right:
Soak artichokes in plenty of lemon juice to prevent them from oxidizing.
  Open them in the centre to make space for the filling. If artichokes are at the end of their season, they may have a 'beard' that also needs removing.
  Fill artichokes with a couple of teaspoons of breadcrumb mixture.

Carciofi fritti
Fried artichokes

There is only one away to eat fried artichokes and that is straight out of the frying pan with a dash of sea salt. In Menfi, as we sip a glass of wine around the kitchen table, to my mother's dismay they disappear even before the next batch is cooked. If they are not very tender, try partially boiling them before coating them with flour.

Serves 4

3 medium-sized artichokes cleaned and prepared
    (see Artichokes stuffed with raisins and pine nuts, page 176)
1 cup of semolina flour
2 cups extra virgin olive oil for frying

Remove artichokes from lemon and water and cut into wedges. Drain and dry.

Pour flour on a plate and coat the wedges.

In a deep pan or wok, bring olive oil to frying temperature and fry the artichoke wedges without overcrowding, turning regularly until golden. Drain on paper towels, sprinkle with salt and serve hot.

See floured and fried artichokes on pages 180 and 181.

This dish featured often at grandmother's lunches. My Aunt Luisa is the only one in the family who still makes it. 'You can't miss this one out of your book', she insisted. To tell the truth, with all my concern about calories, I almost forgot how good this combination is, thanks to the delicious mayonnaise made with pungent extra virgin olive oil. That little extra you make will just disappear over a slice of bread.

Serves 4

3 potatoes, medium-sized
2 lemons
4 or 5 artichokes
2 eggs
2 cups extra virgin olive oil
1 tablespoon parsley, finely chopped

Boil the potatoes in salted water until tender. Drain, cool, peel and cut into cubes about the same size as the artichokes.

In the meantime, prepare a bowl of water with the juice of one lemon and the lemon halves. Clean the artichokes by chopping off the hard outer leaves. Cut off top part where soft and cut into quarters. Wipe with lemon juice and cover with water and lemon to prevent them from browning.

Bring a medium-sized stockpot of water to boil, add a bit of salt and cook the artichokes with the lemons. Check with a skewer in the heart of the artichoke. When soft, drain and leave to cool.

To make the mayonnaise, separate the yolks from the egg whites. Pour yolks in the mixing bowl of a food mixer. Turn the mixer to medium–high speed and slowly pour in the olive oil, drop by drop, until eggs have doubled in volume and mixture has turned a very light yellow. Add salt and lemon juice to taste.

Once ready, alternate the artichoke (which must be well drained) with the potatoes on a serving dish and coat abundantly with the mayonnaise. Sprinkle with parsley and serve at room temperature.

This can be made in advance and refrigerated. Bring back to room temperature before serving.

Insalata di limoni
Lemon salad

Different to orange salad, lemon salad is reminiscent of poor farmers eating what they could. Not too bad considering the amount of vitamins that lemons contain. A few years ago, I was expecting a group of Danes for a quick olive oil tasting in mid January. It was cold, wet and I could not think of anything that could lift spirits in that gloomy weather. 'Make a good lemon salad,' my father suggested. My immediate reaction was 'madness!' However, as I often end up following his suggestions, I made the salad with the addition of a few lettuce leaves. It was such a success that I put it on the menu of my Sicilian dinner at Enoteca Norio in Tokyo the following month.

Serves 4

3 sweet lemons
6 lettuce leaves
spring onion, if available
sea salt
¼ cup extra virgin olive oil

Peel the lemons carefully removing the bitter white pith. Cut into halves and slice. If lemons are a bit sharp, keep them in water and salt for about ten minutes. Drain before using.

Tear lettuce leaves and mix in a bowl in an equal proportion to the lemons. Top with finely sliced spring onion and season with salt and olive oil until well combined.

Fish and meat

Ragù di maiale di Casa Ravidà
Our pork ragout

This dish is made at least once a year, usually towards the end of the winter when we get good ricotta. It simmers in a clay pot for a good eight hours and is mainly used to season pasta. The sundried tomato paste—*estratto*—gives it a rich and intense flavour. Do not be put off by some of the meat cuts used. They are absolutely necessary for the final succulent taste of this ragout we have been making for generations. You will also be surprised how little fat there is in it.

Serves 8-10

200g (½lb) sundried tomato paste
1 onion, chopped
1 twig rosemary
4 sage leaves
2 bay leaves
400g (12oz) of pork belly
600g (1¼lb) of pork meat
600g (1¼lb) of thick pork sausage
a piece of rind with the skin
a pig's trotter
a pig's tail
500ml (16fl oz) tomato sauce
1 cup red wine
400g (12oz) rigatoni or home made tagliatelle
1 to 2 cups fresh ricotta
extra virgin olive oil

Dilute tomato paste in a cup of warm water and pour on a large clay or other pot where you plan to make the ragout. Add the onion, herbs and warm over medium heat.

Seal meat juices by browning all pieces of pork, except the sausage, in a large pan with the olive oil over high heat. Add to the tomato sauce as they are ready. Pour the cup of red wine over the last batch, deglaze all the juices, and add to the meat. Cover with at least 1.7 litres of water, bring to the boil and then lower heat to a soft simmer. Cook for at least eight hours. Check and stir occasionally. Halfway through cooking, season with the salt.

In the meantime, cook the sausage in a pan with 1 cup of water until partially done and add to the rest of the meat, cooking for one more hour before switching off.

When the ragout is almost ready, check that the sauce has a dense creamy consistency. If not, increase heat and reduce. Now remove all pieces of meat and pour sauce through a colander to remove all small bones and other bits and pieces.

The meat is usually served as a second course and only a few tiny bites are added to the pasta sauce.

Cook the pasta according to package directions and drain well. Pour back into a stockpot and season generously with the sauce over medium high–heat, then add about half the ricotta .

Pour pasta onto a large serving dish and top with remaining ricotta and the odd small pieces of meat.

Serve immediately.

Spanish and French influences blend in this recipe. It can also make two dishes, as the onion sauce is used with pasta and then the meat is served with peas and carrots as a second course. In our family it has always been called *Carne alla spagnola* and the pasta seasoned with its delicious onion sauce is called *Pasta con la glace*. It is a popular Sunday lunch as you can make a first and second course in one go.

Serves 4

Place meat in a deep casserole with all the ingredients, top with about 3 litres (5 pints) of water and bring to the boil. Cover with a lid, leaving it slightly ajar and cook over medium–high heat for 1 hour and 45 minutes. Boiling point should be lively but not too high.

Test meat with a skewer and increase heat to reduce juices and glaze the onions as the meat starts to feel soft. As the water dries out, lower heat to prevent the sauce from burning. If the meat is already well cooked, put it aside and continue to reduce the sauce until onions are shiny and glazed. You may need to add a bit of water to obtain perfect glazing. Remove herbs and partially puree the onions in a food processor or chop finely with a knife.

Cool meat, remove string, and cut into thin slices. Line slices side by side in a serving dish. Warm the onion sauce and pour some over the meat.

Reserve or use remaining onion sauce as a pasta sauce.

Right: *Pasta con la glace.*

As soon as cold winter days settle in, our first thought is to have a *salsiccia*, thin sausage with wild fennel seeds. Our butcher makes it daily but we make sure he makes it for us, in front of us, with our own choice of meat cuts and our own fennel seeds. Most people ask the butcher for lean *salsiccia*, with chillies and powdered fennel, finely ground … not as it used to be. We ask for *grassa, molto grassa*—fat, very fat—so that it can brown in its own juices. This is my grandfather's recipe, religiously followed by our butcher. We serve it with boiled vegetables, with *patate a spezzatino*, or fried artichokes, (page 178) on the side.

Serves 4

natural lamb casing, 24mm (1 inch) wide
1kg (2lb) pork meat, meat to belly and gumi meat
20g (¾oz) salt
½ teaspoon black pepper
1 tablespoon wild fennel seeds
2 cups white wine

Soak the casings in water until soft. Grind the meat with an 8mm (¼in) grinder and mix with the salt, pepper and wild fennel seeds until well combined.

Fit a piping bag with a nozzle and attach the casing to it. Fill with the sausage meat and squeeze into the casing in one whole sausage.

Coil the sausage, secure with two long skewers and prick to release fat. Place in an iron skillet, cover with about a cup of water and bring to the boil. Lower heat and simmer until all the water evaporates, about 15 minutes. It is important that the sausage releases all its fat in cooking. Pour in 1 cup of the wine, turn once, and reduce heat to a bare minimum. Continue to cook the sausage in its own fat, turning regularly, until it begins to brown. This can take up to 30 minutes. The longer it takes the tastier.

Raise the heat, add remaining wine, deglaze and pour the juices over the sausage before serving.

Our butcher makes *salsiccia* on demand following my grandfather's recipe.
Salsiccia is coiled and pricked with a skewer so that it can release the fat during cooking.

Cacio all'argentiera is named after a silversmith whom, according to legend, having fallen into poverty, found solace in eating this simple but tasty cheese snack every day.

Cacio all'argentiera
Silversmith's cheese

My great grandmother, Maria Zalapj, came from Piana degli Albanesi, a Greek orthodox area where they still speak a Greek dialect. She apparently loved good, sturdy food. My father likes to recall how, well into her eighties, she would sit for dinner and call the maid to ask what the menu was for that evening. My grandmother would interfere and suggest 'Some lightly boiled vegetables, mother?' or, ' A soup?'... Everyone joined in to propose something apt for an elderly woman's dinner. After many refusals Maria Zalapj would take in a deep breath and with apparent disdain ask for some *Cacio all'argentiera*. It is not exactly the lightest of foods but I love it and occasionally have it for lunch with a nice slice of bread to dip in the oil.

Serves 4

4 cups extra virgin olive oil
4 slices of pecorino cheese, about 1½ cm (1in) thick
16 black olives
oregano
red wine vinegar

Coat a heatproof shallow dish with the olive oil and place one slice of cheese next to the other. Add the olives, oregano and sprinkle with vinegar.

Cook in a preheated oven at 180°C (350°F) Gas Mark 4 or over medium heat with a lid until cheese is soft. Serve immediately.

Bistecca panata
Pan-fried steak coated with breadcrumbs

Meat in Sicily can be good but is certainly not exceptional and probably was less so in the past. This could explain why it is often seasoned or filled with breadcrumbs. This is the quintessential Sicilian steak and my son Alfredo eats it often.

120g (4oz) slice of steak or sirloin per person
¼ cup extra virgin olive oil
50g (2oz) parsley, finely chopped
black pepper
¼ cup tablespoons breadcrumbs, per slice

Coat each slice of meat with about half the olive oil, parsley or oregano and pepper and marinate on a plate, turning occasionally for at least 10 minutes. The meat must be oily to absorb the breadcrumbs.

Put the breadcrumbs in a medium-sized plate or tin. Add the steaks and pat thoroughly with the mixture on both sides until well coated.

Warm an iron pan with remaining olive oil (or use remaining oil from the marinade) and cook over medium heat for about 2 minutes per side, depending on thickness. Pour a tiny bit of olive oil on the meat before turning, as this will toast the breadcrumbs. Season with salt to taste and serve hot.

Desserts

Biancomangiare
Milk pudding

This pudding has a mild aroma of almonds and lemon zest and is traditionally Sicilian. Today, it is also made with milk and topped with cinnamon and pistachios.

Makes 4 x 125ml bowls

200g (7oz) almonds, toasted
2 large strips of lemon zest
20g (¾oz) wheat starch
80g (3oz) sugar
1 tablespoon dark chocolate, finely chopped
cinnamon powder

Toast the almonds in the oven and crush to a coarse powder with a mortar and pestle or food processor. Wrap in a piece of cheese cloth and simmer in ½ litre (1 pint) of water until water turns white. Infuse with the lemon zest.

Mix the sugar with the wheat starch in a saucepan and gradually whisk in the almond water and lemon zest. Stir constantly over medium to low heat, with a wooden spoon making sure the bottom does not burn. Bring to a boil and switch off as soon as custard coats the spoon.

Pour into 4 individual bowls or a single serving bowl.

Top with the finely chopped chocolate and a dash of cinnamon.

Leave to cool or refrigerate until ready to serve.

Next page: Milk pudding made with almonds
and lemon zest is traditionally Sicilian.

Arance affettate con mandorle tostate
Sliced oranges with toasted almonds

We eat a lot of fresh fruit instead of desserts at the end of a meal. When oranges abound, a drop of marsala and a topping of toasted almonds or chopped pistachios suddenly turns them into a colourful last minute dessert.

Serves 4

3 to 4 oranges, depending on size
⅓ cup dry marsala
1 tablespoon sugar
1½ tablespoons pistachios or toasted almonds, chopped

Peel the oranges, removing all the white pith and maintaining their round shape. Cut into even, round ½cm (¼in) slices. Place one next to the other on a round serving dish. Sprinkle with the sugar and the marsala and let rest at least half an hour.

Top with the pistachios or toasted almonds before serving.

Winter buffets feature a feast of different chilled fruit puddings. Make these at least a day in advance.

Serves 4 or makes 15 tangerine halves, depending on size

Cut all the tangerines in half and squeeze. Reserve around 15 of the best halves to refill with the pudding. Rub the juice through a sieve over a bowl and discard the pulp.

Soften the gelatine in a small bowl of warm water for about five minutes.

In the meantime, choose the best tangerine halves and clean off any white threads and piths.

Pour the tangerine juice in a medium-sized stockpot and mix in the sugar, stirring constantly over medium heat. Squeeze excess water from the gelatine and dissolve sheets in the hot juice. Switch off as soon as the juice nears the boil.

Fill each tangerine with a ladle of juice and leave to cool and settle on a flat surface. Then refrigerate for at least 24 hours. Serve cold.

If you have moulds, wet a mould with water and fill with the juice. Cool and refrigerate for at least 24 hours.

Before serving, turn mould onto a round dish and keep refrigerated until ready to use. Decorate with tangerine leaves and finely chopped pistachios or toasted almonds.

This is delicious with a cup of black coffee or at the end of a meal.

Serves 4

125g (4oz) plain flour
½ teaspoon salt
½ teaspoon sugar
75g (2½oz) butter, cold and cubed
2 tablespoons cold water
For the custard:
Juice and zest from 1 lemon
3 eggs
100g (3½oz) sugar
30g (1oz) butter

Sift the flour into a bowl or a food processor. Add the salt and sugar and blend in the cold butter. Gradually add the water, without overworking, until dough holds together. Wrap with plastic film and chill for half an hour.

Warm oven to 180°C (350°F) Gas Mark 4.

Peel the zest from one lemon and cut into very fine strips avoiding any of the white bitter pith. Squeeze the juice from the two lemons and strain through a sieve, to obtain just over ½ cup of juice.

Grease a round 18cm (7in) pie tin with butter or cover with baking paper. Roll out the dough and unroll over the pie tin shaping it around the seam of the tin. Cover the base with baking paper, top with baking beans and cook for 20 minutes or until it begins to colour.

In the meantime, place the eggs, sugar and butter in a small saucepan over a bain-marie. Mix constantly with a wooden spoon over low heat. If custard begins to curdle, bring the heat down. Remove and whisk until smooth. When the sauce just begins to thicken, stir in the juice. Cream will thin again. Add the lemon zest and switch off the heat.

Remove beans from tart, add the custard and cook for a further 10 to 12 minutes or until it has settled. Cool on a rack and serve at room temperature.

Index